Also by Gretel Ehrlich

TRILOGY

In the Empire of Ice
The Future of Ice
This Cold Heaven

MEMOIR

A Match to the Heart

NARRATIVE NONFICTION/TRAVEL

The Solace of Open Spaces
Islands, the Universe, Home
Questions of Heaven

FICTION

Heart Mountain
Drinking Dry Clouds

BIOGRAPHY

John Muir, Nature's Visionary

POETRY

Arctic Heart
To Touch the Body
Geode/Rock Body

CHILDREN'S

A Blizzard Year

Facing the Wave

Facing the Wave

A Journey in the Wake of the Tsunami

Gretel Ehrlich

Pantheon Books, New York

Grateful acknowledgment is made to the following for permission to
reprint previously published material: Columbia University Press:
Excerpt from *Old Taoist: The Life, Art and Poetry of Kodojin* by Stephen
Addiss. Copyright © 2000 by Columbia University Press. Reprinted by
permission of Columbia University Press. · HarperCollins Publishers:
Excerpt from "Die while you live!" from *The Roaring Stream: A New Zen
Reader,* edited by Nelson Foster and Jack Shoemaker. Copyright © 1996
by Nelson Foster and Jack Shoemaker. Foreword copyright © 1996 by
Robert Aitken. Reprinted by permission of HarperCollins Publishers.

Library of Congress Cataloging-in-Publication Data

Ehrlich, Gretel.
Facing the wave : a journey in the wake of the tsunami / Gretel Ehrlich.
p.   cm.
Includes bibliographical references.
ISBN 978-0-307-90731-8
1. Tohoku Earthquake and Tsunami, Japan, 2011.   2. Tsunami
damage—Japan—Tohoku Region.   3. Tsunami relief—Japan—Tohoku
Region.   4. Disaster victims—Japan—Tohoku Region.   I. Title.
CG222.J3E47 2012   363.34'94095211—dc23   2012020400

www.pantheonbooks.com

Jacket design by Ben Wiseman
Book design by M. Kristen Bearse
Maps by Mapping Specialists

Printed in the United States of America
First Edition
2 4 6 8 9 7 5 3 1

For Neal

There are two journeys
in every odyssey, one on worried water,
the other crouched and motionless, without noise.

——DEREK WALCOTT

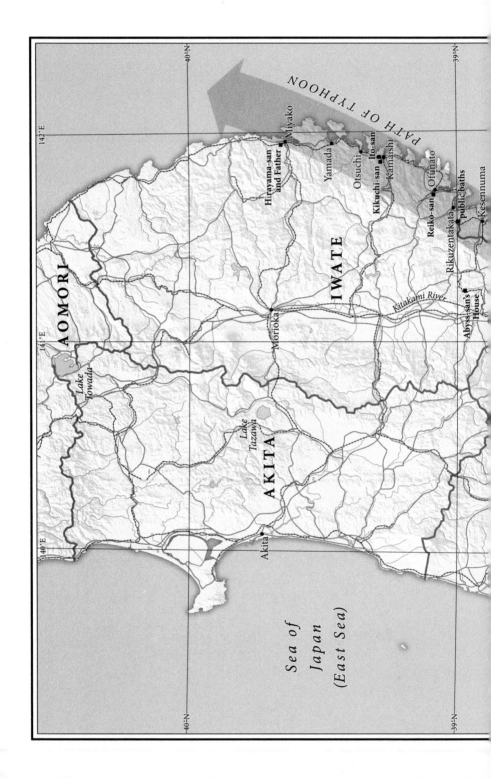

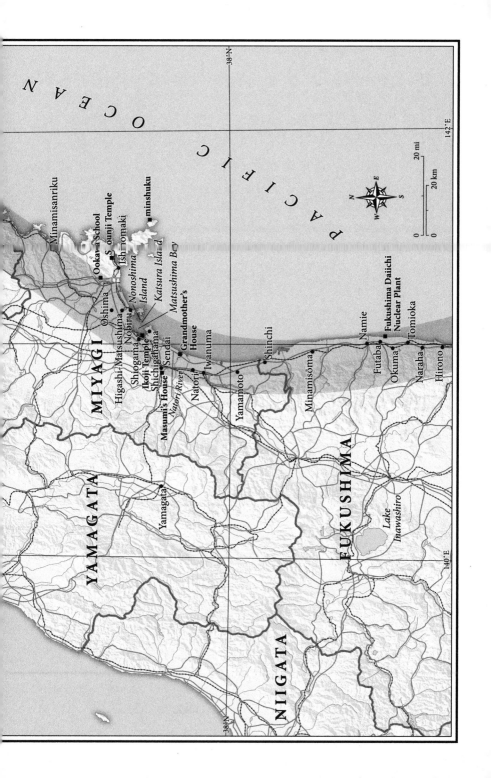

Facing the Wave

The Swimmer

Mizu no michi. The Path of Water. How one swims in it and what it teaches along the way. A wave rises from a seismic rip in the seafloor. It spreads out low and travels at jet speed, mounding up as it hits shore. In Kamaishi, Japan, a forty-year-old fisherman is caught by the first thirty-foot-high tsunami wave to enter the narrow harbor after the 9.0 earthquake that hit northeastern Japan that March 11 day.

Kikuchi-san was driving when his car was almost shaken off the road. Six minutes later, he turned toward his parents' house to rescue them, knowing that a tsunami would come, but his father was going the other way, bicycling toward the harbor.

"Don't go there," Kikuchi-san yelled out, but the elderly man didn't hear. By the time Kikuchi-san caught up with him, his father had climbed the seawall and was clutching a steel ladder, facing the sea.

Kikuchi-san remembers a roar. Water was receding, surging backwards until the ocean floor lay exposed. "We've got to get out of here," Kikuchi-san yelled, but his father didn't move.

The roar intensified. A white line appeared at the horizon. The wave was coming fast. As Kikuchi-san climbed up to get to his father, water came at him. His father shook his head, refusing to budge. One last look, then the young fisherman jumped off the wall. When he turned back, his father was gone. "My father chose to stay, and in that second I accepted it, and thought it would be the same for me too."

Water towered over him. He saw a nine-ton squid boat teetering on the wave's crest, its glass attractor lamps swinging and shattering. The Wave swept him into the river that splits the town of Kamaishi in half. He climbed onto a metal roof, but the water caught him there too, sucking him backwards, pulling him out to sea. The water roiled. It was black with diesel and gas, sewage, dirt, and blood, and Kikuchi-san rolled and thrashed inside its debris-marbled night.

The collapsed wave took the fisherman all over the place. Heavy house beams and pieces of boats slammed into him. He grabbed a breath, went down, and shot up again. Shattered roof tiles skittered by. Water surged and retreated. Another wave drove him deeper, then tossed him sideways and up. He remembers seeing two concrete pillars zoom by as he was pulled under the bridge. His head broke water: he could breathe.

A piece of plastic buoy appeared and he grabbed it. "Retreating water took me back out and another wave carried me in again," he told me. Dead bodies were floating, parts of houses catapulted, cars tumbled, a floating roof banged into a bridge and flipped on its side. The present was splintered. He was lost in a lost world.

"The wave came into the river behind the station. I must have been swept up from the ocean into it, past the petrol station." As the first wave flattened out, the roaring stopped. He remembers silence. Because he could hear, he knew he was alive, not dreaming. "I was stranded in the debris. I couldn't go anywhere. It was so quiet, I heard a dog whimpering somewhere, but couldn't see it. It was so sad." He was brokenhearted, and like the dog, thought he would die.

There was a roar. He looked: a wave was coming back again. Water covered him and he was driven toward one of the bridge pillars. He saw a rope dangling. "I barely got to the pillar before the ocean began dragging me back, so I reached for the rope and grabbed it. My lower half was submerged. Debris was being pulled out, but I kept holding on. As the water drew away, my legs were pulled out in front of me. I was holding tight, floating on my back with my head up. At first I wasn't worried about losing my grip, but then, my hands got very cold."

Water came in false tidal sequences. Between waves, he remembers another period of stillness. "The sea was a lagoon. A log floated past. I climbed onto it." Sitting astride the dead tree he could see the extent of the destruction for the first time. The entire port had been demolished. Fishing boats had been hurled onto the tops of buildings. He lost his boat. Almost every house was gone, including his own. A beam floated by; he was swimming in the remnants of his past.

As the water retreated, he lay on top of the log and paddled toward land. With mud and debris under his feet, he stood, and realized the wave had taken his pants: he was naked. "There was nothing I could do," he said. He saw people standing on a huge mountain of coal and climbed up to join them. A woman yelled, "There's another wave coming." He thought he would die this time, but the water never reached them. He remembers standing there, shivering, for a long time.

Finally he saw that the Kamaishi Port office building was still standing. "The third floor looked okay, so I went that way. I took off my jacket and tied it around my waist. I saw another sweater sticking out of the window of a wrecked car, so I tied it around my backside."

Kikuchi-san swam and stumbled through rubble. He doesn't remember how long it took. In a town of more than 39,000 people, 935 had already died. He crawled into the third-story window. There were 40 people inside. They tried to warm him. He was hypothermic and bleeding; they administered first aid and pulled a pair of gloves over his feet.

A woman he knew came to his side. They didn't speak. Together they watched the sky grow dark. With no city lights on they saw bright stars. Someone lit candles. Desks were pushed together so he could lie on them. The night seemed peaceful; the tsunami, a dream. But the continuous aftershocks jolted him into an understanding of what had happened, and he wondered if his family was alive. When he woke, it was morning.

Up on the roof he looked out on a flattened city. He knew he had to join the throngs wandering through the debris. It was hard to move but he found a stick to use as a cane. Back across the rough plain of wreckage, he climbed up to the bridge. His wife passed him and their eyes met, but she only nodded. When she spoke it was to tell him that their sixteen-year-old daughter was still missing.

They set off to look for her. A few hours later, a fisherman stopped them, and said he'd seen the girl, that she was working with the city firemen who were giving first aid to tsunami victims. For the first time since the disaster, Kikuchi-san cried.

Later, he found his mother at an evacuation center. He kneeled in front of her and quietly told her that her husband had been washed off the seawall. She shook her head and said nothing.

In the next two days, Kikuchi-san went to find his father's body. Fierce aftershocks continued. He dragged his aching body across the ruins of the town. His house was gone; he had seen only a few other fishermen. Many had taken their boats out to sea. He didn't know who was dead and who was alive.

A temporary morgue had been set up in a school gym for unidentified bodies. Kikuchi-san found body #59, and a written description of his father. He unzipped the body bag. His father's watch was still ticking but the man's lungs had filled with seawater, and his heart had stopped. He was sixty-nine years old.

"He spent his whole life on the water," Kikuchi-san said. "And even though it took him, I love the sea; it's all I have."

June

June

The more I lose the happier I am.

—KAZUYOSHI OTOMO

From under a thin futon on tatami that no longer smells like grass, I hear the rattle of shoji screens until a seismic wave carries the house forward and upward in a hard jolt—a slice of contained chaos—and drops it again, down the face of a geologic wave to Earth's uncertain crust.

Masumi's cell phone sounds an alarm. "*Jishin!*" she cries out—earthquake—and rushes fast for the stairs. There's a thud and the roaring noiseless noise that follows, drilling deep inside the ear, deeper than touch, almost beyond hearing. A dog barks. In the distance the tsunami-warning siren sounds. It's dawn on the western outskirts of Sendai.

By the time Masumi, her parents, and I gather downstairs the shaking has stopped, but Kazuko, Masumi's mother, is still holding the kitchen cabinets shut with one outstretched arm. Since the big quake and tsunami on March 11, which devastated almost four hundred miles of Japan's northeastern coast and caused the cooling apparatus of the Fukushima Daiichi power plant to fail, resulting in three hydrogen explosions and the massive nuclear meltdowns in four nuclear reactors, she's replaced broken dishes three times and now keeps the house stocked with bottled water and extra food.

"It wasn't much but . . . " Masumi begins. Her mother finishes the sentence: "It's still scary." She dispenses green tea from a large thermos into small cups. We drink in silence. Tectonic plates are always locking up, warping Earth's crust and moving, and a prediction has been floating around that another big earthquake is coming, and Japan's northeast coast, called Tohoku, will be ravaged again by a tsunami.

Upstairs I roll up my futon. The smell of green tea, coffee, rice, and fried eggs wafts through the small house, mixing with the savage beauty of geological violence that continues to take place. There have been over eight hundred aftershocks greater than 4.5 since March, and it's only June now. In the hallway Masumi confides that, so far, she's been unable to take photographs of the destruction.

Masumi is thirty-five, long-limbed and high-strung; she came back to her parents' house after a ten-year stint in western Canada to get her doctorate in photography. "I should be taking pictures, but it feels like an invasion, like going somewhere I shouldn't go," she says.

Another aftershock comes. Masumi braces herself, and flees downstairs. This is my first time staying in a modern Japanese house with neon lights and a living room full of Western furniture, and as things rattle, I long for the recesses of dark rooms and deep eaves, where the shaking of Earth is also the shaking of shadows, where what Jun'ichiro Tanizaki called "the laws of darkness" are stirred.

* * *

On March 11, 2011, Japan's earth-altar broke. The descending oceanic plate—a slab of lithosphere—slid under the overlying plate that carries the island of Honshu. Pulling and grinding, the subduction zone was pulverized. Its topmost plate bulged and dropped, and a rupture occurred: an undersea rip, 6 feet across, 310 miles long, and 120 miles wide.

Friction is stress; stress is energy. The earth moved. A wave was born. Three sorrows: quake, tsunami, meltdown. In the quake's "seismic moment," the total energy released was two hundred thousand times the energy at the earth's surface, equal to six hundred million times the energy of the bomb dropped at Hiroshima. In six shaking minutes the northeastern coast of Japan was torn off its roots with an undersea roar that could be heard on hydrophones in Oregon.

Seismic waves are not tidal. There is no moon-pulling or wind pushing involved. They occur when ocean-floor earthquakes displace seawater at the fractured fault line. The first thing to reach the coast is the trough, what might be called "the emptiness aspect of the wave." The drawback is severe: the ocean floor is bared. The backed-up water is a fist ready to spring, and when the waves finally arrive, their kinetic energy packs a punch equal to, say, seventeen hundred pounds in the face. Forward-rolling, they drag bottom all the way. Upon entering shallow water, they slow suddenly, the water behind piling up, and grow to a tremendous height.

Legends about tsunamis describe them as "whirling waves of foam." This wave was a mist-spitting, white-crested monster that pulled back fast and drove forward, breaking its own legs, and collapsing onto more than three hundred miles of shore.

The curtain in Masumi's living room fills with wind and empties out. "Have you noticed that *jishin*—earthquakes—usually come when there's changing weather?" Masumi asks. Outside, the sky is a pale sheet veined with radioactive rainclouds. They are gray, layered with black, and hang over the sacred mountains to the west, then darken the Sendai Plain with a tattered fringe. A hefty downpour begins.

In the origin myths of Japan, Izanagi and Izanami stand on the floating bridge of heaven looking down. They are lonely. His swinging phallus drips; her oceanic vulva opens and they are joined. The progeny of their union is at first terrestrial: the eight large islands of Japan. Then gods appear: the goddess of the sun, the god of the moon, and the emperor. Divine creatures lived in an undersea palace with pillars of jade and gates of pearl, carpets of sealskin and silk, its spirit-filled, imperial beginnings seemingly inviolate. Many earthquakes, wars, and tsunamis later, this island nation felt its vulnerability.

Tohoku, the northeastern region of the island of Honshu, was affected by the tsunami from Sendai north to Hachinohe, about thirteen hundred kilometers. Its "bridge of heaven" was clobbered by a wave, its furnishings and population ground down to fantastic shapes. Every morning I wake to the unfamiliar: wave-like aftershocks rise to the second floor of the house. Every morning I wonder where I am. The constant jolts and shakes remind me that this isn't my country, my culture, or my disaster. Yet, since my first trip to Japan in 1968, I've returned many times. When I heard about the tsunami on the radio, I came as soon as I could, though I'm not sure why. Maybe, just to walk Tohoku's charnel ground; to meet those who faced the wave and survived.

Soft rain falls on Kazuko's garden shrine, a miniature Shinto temple glazed red with a curved tile roof. Two cups have been placed on its tiny veranda: one for water, one for salt. Water to make the household harmonious, salt to scare the bad spirits away. With so many dead and missing—approximately twenty thousand so far—Tohoku is swarming with ghosts.

The list of Japan's seismic events dates back to the year 684. Japanese ideas about religion, architecture, theater, and literature are based on *wa* and *shunyata*—concepts of plentitude and uncertainty, of togetherness framed by impermanence. "Every time there's an aftershock, a tremor, my grandmother's mind shakes into coherence, into wisdom. Every time the earth shakes she gets better," Masumi tells me.

* * *

Masumi was driving when the 9.0 earthquake hit. After the early warning alert on her cell phone sounded she turned on her wide-screen GPS, also a television, and watched the tsunami as it was happening. A police helicopter filmed the Sendai coast where the Natori River empties out: she watched her old neighborhood wash away. "I saw waves coming," she said. "I saw my uncle's rice fields disappear, and the trees at the coast break in half. I saw where water had pushed my grandmother's house until it came apart. I saw the roof floating."

Getting home from Tohoku University to the western side of Sendai took hours. Roads had buckled and bridges were ripped apart by the force of the waves. There were traffic jams: people rushing away from the coastal areas, and hurrying back to see if their houses had survived. Another 7.0 aftershock made her car "buck like a horse." More quakes came. Streets and rice fields were flooded. Water was knee-deep. It started to snow.

"Two pilots in training were returning to Sendai Airport just after the tsunami occurred," she told me. "The tower, operating on backup generators, told the planes to turn back. The pilots asked why. Ground Control replied: 'The Sendai Airport no longer exists.' "

Masumi drove the long way around Sendai as if trying to regain lost microseconds. Speed × Time: what did it mean? The Tohoku earthquake had altered time, and caused the axis of the earth to shift ten inches. The planet's moment of inertia had been shaken loose. The earthquake was inertia in action: what inertia does when it dances. Earth spun faster and days were shortened. Perhaps it will keep spinning harder and harder until there are no days at all.

Along every water-logged road Masumi traveled on the way home there were obstructions. The Tohoku coast had dropped vertically two feet, allowing flood water to stand and not drain, and the narrow harbor and river openings invited the wave to intrude inland as much as six miles. Roads were also rivers, and rivers ingested salt. The Wave was time pouring onto shore, the future moving into the present, invading houses, taking lives, and ordering the warped world into an unstable *now*.

Wave follows wave. They can be crust or else water. It's thought that a quake like this can jar the planet into what's known as "free vibration," setting up new kinds of terrestrial wave rhythms. Earth is not water, but bell. The tsunami proved it: the sea's wet clapper made Earth ring.

Masumi's drive took longer because the planet's mass had been redistributed, as if mass and mantle were currencies. She'd thought Honshu was a solid place, but between the moment the cell phone alert sounded and the beginning of her drive home, the width of the island increased by almost eight feet, and near the epicenter of the quake, the seabed shifted seventy-nine feet.

By the time Masumi arrived home, no one on the Tohoku coast had heat, water, electricity, or phone service. Unbeknownst to them, the earthquake and the tsunami had knocked out the diesel backup generators that cooled the four operating nuclear reactors at Tokyo Electric Power Company's (TEPCO's) Fukushima Daiichi nuclear power plant, releasing a reported 1.7×10^{19} becquerels of xenon-133, and 3.5×10^{16} becquerels of cesium-137, as well as iodine and strontium.

Between March 11 and 13, the wind was blowing out to sea, but on the morning of March 14, it changed direction, carrying radioactive particles inland, west toward the spine of mountains that dissects Honshu, and north up the devastated coast, passing directly over Sendai, where rain began, intensifying the deposition of radioactive material onto the ground.

Inside their house, Masumi and her parents wrapped themselves in a Pendleton blanket given to her by a Blackfoot Indian in Canada. As it grew colder, they piled on quilts, sheets, and the living room drapes. In preceding days there had been fore-shocks, some as strong as 7.1. Now aftershocks came in sharp spasms, the earth's crustal instabilities making themselves known. Masumi and her parents huddled, cried, and laughed. The sea, the air, and the ground were now drenched with radio-activity. She asked her father, a tall, calm man from a family of alpine skiers, if it was the end of the world, and he smiled, wiped his eyes, and said, "I don't know."

* * *

No fixed points. No shore. Only continual flux, nuclear explo-sions, vented radiation, flooding and flexing, crustal recycling and collapsing, the annihilating heft of water.

Masumi and I have begun to explore the coast where she spent her childhood. Every morning her mother, Kazuko, fills ther-moses with ice water, packs rice balls for lunch, and stuffs our pockets with charms from the sacred mountain of Haguro, plus gloves of garlic and small packages of salt to keep ghosts away. When I ask, why salt? she stares hard at me. "Ghosts don't like it," she says.

Kuruma no michi. The path of the car, or rather, Masumi's bright red 4x4 Toyota. It's the small joke between us, this allusion to the poet Matsuo Bashō's *Oku no Hosomichi, The Narrow Road to the Deep North.* But we're driving, not walking, looking for the living among the dead, so fraught and hypervigilant, we some-times break into hysterical laughter, followed by tears.

A *michi* is a road but can also mean "following the Buddhist way" as well as "a path to a grave"; *kuruma* is "car," and the word *grave* comes from the old French and can also mean "shore."

When Masumi went to search for her relatives who had farmed rice, vegetables, and flowers at the coast for five generations, most roads at the coast were impassable.

Families were split up. Wherever you were when the earthquake hit was where you remained for days. No cell phones worked. She did not know who was dead, who was alive, and, either way, where they might be.

Masumi described her search: "I went first to find my grandmother and my uncle, Kazuyoshi, and his wife. They lived together in my grandmother's house. I drove as far as I could to the coast, but there was so much flooding, I had to get out of the car and run. The water was knee-deep. People had gone to hillside shrines, Buddhist temples, hospitals, government buildings, and schools for safety. Some were saved, some were caught on the roads, some buildings were overtaken by the Wave. Near the Natori River, to be on the second floor wasn't high enough. In other places you had to be on the fourth floor, if there was one. We were all looking for loved ones. People were crying, some were screaming. I kept asking for my grandmother at shelters. Sometimes, people were so grief-stricken, they couldn't talk at all."

Masumi made many stops. At designated evacuation centers photographs of survivors were posted on the walls. That's how she finally found her grandmother—she saw the woman's picture. "She was alone, without family, in an evacuation center. The earthquake knocked her wheelchair over and threw her under a heavy table. That's what saved her, but many others around her died."

It's been one hundred days since the disaster and special prayers are being said for the missing and dead. Even after Buddhism merged with Shinto, old Shinto beliefs prevail in Tohoku to this day: death is an unseemly corruption; ghosts are ubiquitous and to be feared. In ancient times, houses where a death had occurred were abandoned. But the *moya,* the "mourning house," was miniaturized into a replica of a Shinto temple that is kept on a high ledge. Inside were small "spirit-sticks" with the names of the dead engraved on them. Earlier Masumi's mother showed me their two shrines—the one outside in the garden, and the one on top of a closet in her bedroom.

On the way to the rice fields we drive by the Sendai Port. It is a scene of devastation. Big-name factories—Sony, Toyota, Kirin, and Shiseido—are nothing but bent frames with the insides pushed out and scattered. "The press said the Japanese weren't looting, but they were, a little bit," Masumi says. "We just call it gathering up what has been left behind! There were photographs of women running around the Shiseido factory grabbing expensive cosmetics—tanning cream and moisturizers, and sunblock. They were very happy to have those things. And Kirin beer . . . people just helped themselves. After the tsunami, everyone needed a beer!"

Parking lots jammed with workers' cars were crushed in place; acres and acres of cars were lost. "Very Japanese," Masumi says, looking at one such parking lot with a thousand or so ruined cars. "All so neat." But unfixable. "We are all driving very carefully now because there are no Toyota parts."

Slowly, through city traffic, we finally approach the coast, the woman's voice on the GPS instructing: *"Hidari-desu . . . hidari-desu."* Left. Left. Then after we've been driving for two hours, the GPS voice says we should stop and rest, a suggestion we ignore.

Bits of rubbish appear, flung against houses and fences. Rice fields are muddied over with standing water. Around a corner we pass schoolchildren in tidy navy blue uniforms walking home. Men and women ride bicycles, their only form of transportation. In a vacant lot, three uniformed officials are poking sticks into the mud. They no longer look for the living, only for the dead.

Traffic police stop us. They wave their batons so grace-fully they might be conducting a symphony. The road ahead is twisted and a bridge in the distance is out—the entire middle section gone. On the side of the road there's more debris: a coat, a tree branch, five metal light poles bent completely in half, the sixth one standing. The arm of an orange crane moves, piling up a stack of crushed cars. We're motioned ahead, and as we creep along on a temporary gravel track, civilization stops. We enter a wild place of total devastation.

Don't breathe. Don't swallow. Stay covered. Knee boots, gloves, face masks on. I thought it would be black, this tsunami-devastated coast, with a Hokusai wave frozen in place, always arriving, always threatening. But on this June day the Pacific Ocean is flat and blue, the ruined coast is gray dust thick with crematorium ash, and there is no wave.

Yet I see aqueous corruption: the ruined, broken, bloated; the sickening to-and-fro of corpse-thickened water, and ghost-thickened air. An odd smell pervades—one that is hard to pin down. It is decomposing plants, fish, and flesh, and the min-eral smell of bodies being burned; but the radiation that moves through flesh has no scent at all.

For three or four hundred years Masumi's family has grown rice and lived in abundance and wealth, just north of where the Natori River empties into the Pacific Ocean. Once there were rice, flower, and vegetable fields here; now three feet of mud, left behind by the tsunami, is a thick skin that seals the rough corners of these fields, smoothing them, and carrying the vague shine of a midday moon.

We drive on a temporary raised roadbed toward the barren ground where Masumi's grandmother's capacious house once stood. When I open the car window, the noise of heavy equip-ment fills my ear. Mountain-building is ongoing: the flat horizon is being lifted into hills of stacked debris, a word that has come to be a euphemism for the dead, the rotting, the wrecked, and the broken bones of what once stood.

"The Wave came over the seawall there," Masumi says, pointing east. "The wall was useless. The Wave crossed the river and many people were swept away." We pass a small airplane, its battered wing stuck in the mud. Boats ride waves of rice straw. An entire Shinto temple lies crushed under its own heavy roof. We pass a crematorium and stop to read a hastily hand-drawn sign instructing people to carry the bodies through the back door. "One at a time, please, because there are only two stoves working." The wave even washed through the dead, I say to Masumi. A priest is standing where a body has just been wheeled in. He puts his palms together and bows. "They say he comes here every day to pray," she tells me.

In the distance pine trees at the beach are jack-knifed. Some are down and broken into bits. Pieces of seawall are strewn between dead trees. Down a dirt track in what was once a neighborhood of cultivated fields and farmhouses, Masumi stops, clutching the steering wheel. Her head drops. "It's been difficult for me to come here. I feel ghosts all around me," she whispers.

We get out of the car. The foundation of Grandmother's house is all that remains, but curiously, the rock garden that graces the entrance is intact. Orange and pink flowers bloom in the clefts. Toward the ocean her uncle's rice fields are thick with mud and debris, but a single head of lettuce remains—all that's left of the kitchen garden. I kneel down to look: the lettuce is a tiny ball of green, a miniature globe of a lost world.

Objects retrieved from the house have been carefully placed in boxes by the heavy-equipment operators—a tea cup, a rice bowl, and two bags of broken glasses. I ask Masumi why she doesn't take these things home. "No," she says. "I'm not next in line. That's for my uncle or my mother to do."

We adjust our white face masks and walk back to the car. A

small river runs in back of the house. On the other side is the damaged but standing home of her great-aunt and -uncle. "My grandmother always had a view of water, and of her brother." Masumi says. "Now water has taken everything from her."

We go to what's left of a shrine on a tiny hill—a strange bump on the Sendai Plain. Water washed over it and left only two trees. One is a pine, its massive trunk broken in half; the other is smaller and more fragile, a cherry tree. The shrine is gone.

Farmers' and fishermen's families from this neighborhood come here every year in May to pray for their ancestors whose souls are said to live in the *ihai*—long, narrow cedar-wood sticks that bear the names of the dead written in white ink. "The *ihai* are very important to us," Masumi says. "All the ones from here were washed away, including my grandfather's and the ones before his—all five generations. Their *ihai* are gone."

I turn on my heel and look the other way. Far off, a dust cloud blooms and falters. If a large earthquake came now, we'd be in trouble, but there's only the sound of bulldozers reshaping rubble and the blowing banners of dust. The ocean's whitecaps blink and stretch. Then a few rain squalls bump across serrated water until the wind-knife slices pink swells into corrugated fiefdoms.

"The wave washed over this hill," Masumi tells me, "and took the shrine, took everything except this cherry tree. A month after the tsunami—in April—it started blooming. Why did it survive when nothing else did?" Cherry blossoms and death. Strange companions.

> From a hill above
> the ruined coast I watch
> death come into being.
> Blossoms falling.

We speed away from the devastated plain to visit Masumi's grandmother in the hospital. "When I told her how I'd found her after the earthquake, she thought she had become famous because her picture was on the wall," Masumi says. "That's just like her. She's loud and talks too much and she always survives."

The hospital is modern, bright, and clean, with wide windows, as if the traditional Japanese house had been turned inside out—everything exposed now to sun, wind, rain, and radiation. When we walk into her room she appears to be delirious. Her eyes are shut, her breathing heavy. Masumi warned me that her grandmother is sly; that sometimes she pretends to be worse off than she is.

She leans down and whispers into the old woman's ear. "It's me, Masumi." Grandmother opens her eyes and doesn't appear to comprehend. Half an hour later she says, "Who's that *gaijin* with you?"

It's hot in the room so I go to her, unfold my blue, made-in-China fan, and push cool air across her face. She rolls her head from side to side in the breeze. She asks: "Where are we living now? Is my house still standing?"

"No," Masumi whispers in a broken voice. "It's gone."

* * *

Where Kisagata's cherry trees
are buried in waves
A diver rows her boat
Through blossoms

—SAIGYO

Uncle Kazuyoshi

He shakes out a bag of peanuts onto the low table between us, opens four cans of beer, and watches me drink. We sit on the floor and sweat in the midsummer night's heat. The cold stream of liquid feels good going down. We're at Kazuyoshi's house. Masumi's uncle. A farmer, his face is sun-roughened and there's dirt in the deep grooves of his palms. Before the March 11 earthquake hit Kazuyoshi was planting his fields in rice and flowers. He smiles: "I lost everything. Now I feel better."

He grins, drinks, pours two beers and empties more peanuts onto the table between us. Masumi, her mother, and I are in his ground-floor apartment donated by the German company BASF. In the tiny garden space outside he's already planted tomatoes, onions, greens, lettuce, and flowers. He shows me an especially rare kind of Gerber daisy, a spiky miniature red bloom. "I grew these when courting my wife," he tells me. "I delivered buckets-full three times a week until she consented to marry me."

Kazuyoshi squints. Because of a car accident when he was young, he's slightly blind in one eye. In a deep, hoarse voice he says: "Springtime, I used to get in a bad mood. No more. I don't want to be a bother to anyone; I don't want to be a big farmer. Just treat plants and flowers very nicely so my wife and I can survive. If others are happy eating what I grow, then I'm happy." He finishes off a third beer.

The ground begins to shake. Kazuyoshi grabs the edge of the table but doesn't move. Masumi and I jump to our feet. The tsunami siren sounds. We're only a mile from the ocean. Masumi fishes for her car keys, and I gather my notebooks. We stand, all except her uncle. He's scared but calm, or else frozen in place. The shaking subsides.

We sit again. The mood has changed, as well as our heart rates. Kazuyoshi turns serious. He leans forward: "Do you want to hear my story?" Without waiting for an answer, he begins: "On March 11 I was making compost when the *jishin* came. I couldn't stand up, so I sat down on the ground and waited until it stopped."

He drove his tractor to the house and found that the stone lanterns in the garden had fallen, and inside, all the dishes and furniture had broken. He rummaged around and found his money, but when he went outside he saw cars and trucks speeding away. "It must be bad," he thought, and grabbed his wife's hand. They ran for the elementary school, the designated evacuation spot.

"It took a while for the tsunami to arrive. It was about 3:30 or 3:35 when it came. I saw a white splash of water, then something black. Someone screamed, 'Tsunami!' People were struggling to get up the stairs to the third floor. There were maybe two to three hundred people. My wife and I were the last ones there, a little late because I hadn't really thought it would come, and sometimes she's a little slow. Sometimes we both are . . . "

The water charged at them. It was moving about twenty kilometers per hour. They held hands and made it as far as the second floor, but the water flooded in and engulfed them. They were lifted up. Water came up their legs, their arms, their shoulders and necks. Water rose almost to the ceiling.

Chin, cheeks, mouth, nostrils: underwater. Kazuyoshi and his wife had to tilt their heads back just to breathe. "At times we were completely underwater, inhaling filth and getting cold very quickly. We tried everything—paddling fast and feeling for something to put our feet on. We had to concentrate hard. We had to survive."

Four inches of air space kept them alive. Water was lapping their ears. Their heads were back, they were holding hands and treading water; they were waiting to drown. Another wave came. "This is the end of our lives," he told his wife. "It was like being on the *Titanic*," he says, laughing now. "But it wasn't a movie. It was way worse. Real dying! That's what it was!"

He pours another beer and sucks in a deep, vocalized breath as if to assure himself that there is sufficient oxygen in the room. "The wave receded and the next one didn't come close. The water went down and we could see. The staircase to the next floor appeared, as if inviting us! We ran up to the third floor. We had survived, but when I looked out I saw that water covered everything. I saw cars, and bodies, and pine trees floating, I saw that my rice fields were gone, and the family house. The school we were in was the only place left standing. It was an island out at sea."

Another beer and it's time to leave. As we stand, Kazuyoshi hands us four fresh tomatoes, just picked from his tiny garden. He shows us a single head of lettuce: the one that Masumi and I saw near the entrance to her grandmother's house. Kazuko takes an outer leaf and lays it on her tongue—a green wafer emblematic of a lost life. She chews and swallows—it's all that's left of the farm where she grew up.

"Everything needs rescuing," Kazuyoshi says, laughing. There is no mention of the radiation wafting up the coast from Fukushima Daiichi. Reluctantly, Kazuko accepts one of the tomatoes. "This is absurd. You have nothing and you're giving us food," she says. He stares hard at her: "The less I have, the happier I am."

Radiation News

At 2:46 on the afternoon of March 11 the epicenter of the earth-quake occurred forty-five miles east of the Oshika Peninsula at a shallow depth of 19.9 miles, where it damaged the cold-water supply systems at Fukushima Daiichi nuclear power plant. Fifty-one minutes later it was hit by a forty-nine-foot-high tsu-nami wave. Within a week, 580 workers from all over Japan, plus 140 U.S. Marines, were on site, working fifteen minutes at a time inside the buildings, trying to keep the six nuclear reactors from exploding. They failed. Later, the workers told journalists that the buildings moved and jerked so hard, that pipes began coming apart immediately.

Not all waves are made of water. The workers described the earthquake as coming in two intense waves, and by the time the second one started, the pipes inside the Daiichi nuclear power plant that regulate the heat of the reactor and carry coolant to it were bursting open, though TEPCO claimed it was the tsunami that caused the circulatory destruction.

Oxygen tanks exploded, and the wall of the turbine building in reactor 1 cracked. A tangle of overhead pipes buckled. Others jerked away from the walls. Minutes later, but before the tsunami wave hit, the walls of reactor 1 began to collapse. A radiation alarm sounded and white smoke was seen coming from the top of the reactor.

After the first tsunami wave hit the power plant, all the electrical and cooling systems failed. Six hours after the earthquake, radiation levels rose to 0.8 millisieverts—a measure of radiation exposure—every ten seconds: more than a twenty-minute exposure for a human would be fatal.

Five workers died from internal injuries. The Wave bashed the side of reactors 1 and 2 and flooded the basements of the turbine buildings, cutting off all power, including the emergency diesel generators. Though additional backup generators had been installed in watertight hillside buildings, the switching stations that connected backup power to the cooling systems were not watertight, and they failed.

Temperatures rose. Reactors 1, 2, 3, and 4 experienced meltdowns. Water levels dropped in the fuel rod pools stored precariously on top of the reactor buildings. Overheating occurred. Residents of areas within twelve miles of the plant were evacuated. The workers at the power plant stayed, despite repeated exposure to higher levels of radiation than the Japanese government and TEPCO admitted.

Workers attempted to open ventilation valves by hand but failed. One worker heard what he called "an eerie, deep popping noise" from a structure at the bottom of the reactor, and when he propped his foot on it to open the valve, his rubber boot melted from the heat.

That evening, Masao Yoshida, the fifty-six-year-old plant manager, made a decision against the wishes of the TEPCO officials. As a last resort he began pumping seawater into the reactor core, but it was already too late to cool the reactor: hydrogen explosions were about to take place.

Aftershocks kept coming. Workers laid cable in an attempt to restore power, all the while wading in knee-deep water. Fires erupted. At 3:36 p.m. on March 12, a day after the earthquake and tsunami, a hydrogen explosion occurred in reactor 1, blowing away the side walls, leaving only the steel frame. Later, there were explosions in reactors 3 and 4.

Four workers were injured and a fifth was taken to the hospital. Everyone inside and outside of the plant was exposed to extremely high levels of radiation. Daiichi plant chief Masao Yoshida, who kept pouring seawater into the burning heart of the reactors, said: "Many times I thought I was going to die."

"There has been no meltdown," Edano Yukio, a government official, famously announced. But the workers inside, later known as the Fukushima 50, knew otherwise. Requesting anonymity, they said that inspections and repairs to the forty-year-old power plant had not been carried out systematically, and two-year-old reports of water pipe deterioration had been ignored. TEPCO officials later blamed the meltdown solely on the tsunami so as not to appear negligent, but the cover-ups kept coming.

The GE-designed nuclear plant was programmed for a maximum tsunami height of only twenty-one feet, and even that eventuality was not taken seriously. Even at that wave height, seawater might have flooded to a height of forty-nine feet. The shaking of the 9.0 earthquake and the wave that followed exceeded every design specification.

Later reports claim that Fukushima Daiichi nuclear plant released twice as much radioactive material as the government revealed: 35,800 terabecquerels of cesium-137 were emitted during the disaster, not 15,000 terabecquerels as Japan's nuclear regulator announced.

A becquerel (Bq), named after a Frenchman who won the 1903 Nobel Prize in nuclear physics, is a unit of radioactivity, and refers to the activity of a specific quantity of radioactive material in which one nucleus decays per second. A terabecquerel is a multiple of a Bq. One terabecquerel = 10^{12} Bq.

Earthquake damage to the plant may have exacerbated the release of cesium-137 from the pools used to store spent nuclear fuel rods. There was a release of xenon-133 immediately after the earthquake and before the tsunami.

* * *

Evacuations have been expanded from a ten-kilometer-wide perimeter from the Fukushima Daiichi nuclear plant to a twenty-kilometer perimeter referred to as the "no/go zone." Anyone entering will be removed and fined 100,000 yen. Over two hundred thousand residents have been sent to live outside the zone.

One peta = a million, billion becquerels. In thirty years, only half the area's radioactivity will be lost because cesium is a slow-decaying element. Radioactively contaminated rainwater in the runoff has entered the sea.

Emergency response was deemed by the media as "chaotic, slow, inefficient, and peppered with denial and untruths."

Fukushima Daiichi continues to falter. After the plant manager tried to cool the reactors with seawater, one petabecquerel of cesium-137 leaked back into the ocean. It is considered the worst maritime contamination disaster in recorded history.

Every Cove

In the sound of heartbreak there is no form or shadow.

—LI KUNG-LIN

On the Pacific Ocean a single current line moves: a flattened compass needle rides over the cardinal directions as if they didn't exist. I grew up on the other side in California, facing Japan. When the tide pulls out a curtain of gray shakes off light. Asleep or awake, the mind skates. No surface is real.

We're on a family trip—Masumi, her parents, and I—following the highway north to visit the devastated coastal cities north of Sendai. After, Saburo, Masumi's father, insists that we visit a family-owned house in the mountains where Matsuo Bashō once stayed the night. "It's important to keep things in balance," he says. "Too many depressing sights are bad for your health."

A convoy of policemen, lights flashing, passes us. It's a constant sight on every Tohoku road. They have been brought from Hiroshima, Kobe, Tokyo, Shizuoka, Kumamoto—from all over Japan to help with the effort to find missing bodies. Going the other way are vans full of volunteers, some of the 6,600 who have been trained by Peace Boat (among others) to distribute food, shovel mud, and repair graveyards. A dog that had been floating on debris a mile out at sea is rescued; and a baby, swept from its parents' arms, is found alive and reunited with its mother and father. There are four hundred thousand evacuees living in shelters.

As we drive, Saburo tells me about two young cousins, both boys. They were riding in a family car that was swept off the road by the tsunami. The boys swam out of the vehicle holding hands; the parents who were driving did not make it. When a torrent of water separated the cousins, the newly orphaned boy was placed in an evacuation shelter; the other boy made it to his mountain home where he rejoined his family. The orphan had no idea that his cousin was still alive. But in the weeks that followed their separation, his cousin searched for him. Two months later, he found the boy and took him home to live with his family.

We exit the highway and follow a winding coastline of exquisite beauty—as breathtaking as California's Highway 1 in Big Sur. There are almost no other cars. An itinerant priest hugs the side of the road carrying a walking stick, counting the beads of his *juzu* in his right hand. The hem of his robe is covered in mud. He wears white socks and black tennis shoes—no straw sandals for this pilgrim. He's been to Ookawa Elementary School and two Buddhist temples, Kannonji and Shounji, where many of the dead were taken. Now he's walking in the direction of the port town of Ishinomaki, where more than four thousand people died and 80 percent of the houses in the fishing port were destroyed.

The coast is jagged with high rock cliffs. Every cove bears marks of disaster: broken trees, overturned skiffs, and bits of broken houses. Thick forests of *sugi* and *matsu*—cedar and pine—come down to the water. Around another corner we see an entire pulverized village. Behind, in the trees, there's a thirty- to forty-foot-high trimline made by the Wave, a brown watermark, a shadow-line of the wave that killed them.

Every cove. Ravaged, clogged, and tangled with rubbish. A woman's dress hangs from a tree.

* * *

We stop to eat a picnic lunch. "How lucky we are," Masumi says, "to have food." High cliffs, pine-studded rock islets, crashing surf: "*Kanpeki*," I say. Perfect. If we just stood here and didn't move north or south, we might be able to forget. But each bite means we're ingesting radioactive food and air.

To sever all this from the mind—how easy it sounds, delicious in fact; then life would be sweet again, wouldn't it? Or was it ever that way? But it's too late. We're alive and death is real. Like the Buddhist priest who is walking the coast, we too are on some sort of path. No getting off now.

North to Minamisanriku, only eighty kilometers west of the quake's epicenter, a fishermen's town of seventeen thousand where over ten thousand people died. A twenty-four-year-old city worker, Miki Ando, voluntarily took over the public announcement post and on the loudspeaker urged people to go to higher ground. She stayed at her post too long. The Wave was coming fast; at the last moment she climbed to the roof of the building, but it washed her away. Her body was not found until April.

We enter the town in silence. Saburo says, "We need to see it because this is one of the towns that was wholly destroyed." The car transports us but the body carries the eye. We drop down from the coast to a crenulated sea-lane and cross a makeshift, one-lane bridge. The lifeless realm before us has a cockeyed look: a boat on top of a house on top of three crushed cars. We almost laugh, but tears leak from our eyes.

We drive down a stark avenue. On either side there is only rubble. Please slow down, I ask. We're going too fast. It's too difficult to take all this in. But there is no speed slow enough to comprehend.

* * *

A small river winds out of the mountains through a green valley. It leaks, rubble-choked, into this town. We cross a crudely made temporary bridge. From the sea, it was said that the town looked like it was sinking, but down on the flats, the opposite is true: the height of the rubble is as tall as the Wave.

Masumi and I get out of the car and walk. The red steel frame of the city building where Miki Ando died still stands, but nothing else of it remains. Only the mayor survived: he climbed the cell phone tower atop the roof; tried, but couldn't save the others. Beneath his feet, thirty-three coworkers, including Miki, were swept away.

Closer to the harbor is a four-story hospital where the Wave blasted through the first-, second-, and third-story windows and doors. An X-ray machine dangles from an opening, as does a nurse's uniform. Two hundred people were rescued from the roof, but the rest of the patients, doctors, and nurses died. The Wave turned a place of safety into a killing field, squandering needed medicines and erasing all records of what had happened to whom and when and why. A fishing boat is perched on top of the hospital's second-floor terrace.

We turn from the hospital and look out on a plain of chaos, a monstrous collage that no eye, no painting could truly capture. No one object is whole and no city remains. All is a broken scramble, the sum total of which is an intricate blank. Blank because it no longer carries the constructs of everyday life, of a functioning town.

It's oddly quiet. Wind pushes radioactive dust into our eyes. The crushed and the silent and the surreal. Two hundred days ago it was a thriving fishing port; one hundred days ago it was a horrific theater of disaster. From north to south, from Hachinohe to Hirono, roughly 365 miles were taken by water; over two hundred thousand buildings destroyed. Now there are only twisted remnants. No matter how I look at it, there is nothing and everything for the eye.

* * *

To say rubble
isn't enough.
Night cannot cover it.
A bird flies.

Ishinomaki

Water is heavy. After being displaced at the rupture site it becomes a moving mass whose fluidity is like something solid. Yet it slips and slides, shoves and gathers. It splits the ends of things, fills and empties them, and carves new shapes that are blunt, tipping, and as sharp as knives.

At the port of Ishinomaki a fisherman stands in front of his boat, its bow piercing the second story of a house. A piece of tatami juts out from the front door. Broken dishes lie in the street. His arms are folded. He stands and stares. Around him, the sky darkens. Then a curtain of black rain begins to fall. It pours down on him. He doesn't run for cover. More than three thousand people in this city died in one day.

Everything is black. Black water rising, dirt roads drinking it in. Row after row of narrow fishermen's houses are bent, crushed, and battered by what must have been water-hurled fishing boats and debris. We move through murk and ink. In the spring of 1689, when the wandering poet Matsuo Bashō set off to search the far north as well as the inner regions of his mind, he lost his way and emerged from the forest at Ishinomaki. Even then, it was a thriving seaport not much to his liking. He wrote: "Hundreds of merchant ships were gathered in the bay. In the town, houses fought for space, and smoke rose continuously from the salt-kilns. I thought to myself, I never intended to come anywhere like this . . . We looked for lodgings for the night but were refused by everyone." What would Bashō write now on this page of destruction?

* * *

An aftershock rattles the car windows. Though the road has been made two feet higher, it isn't enough. At high tide water splashes against the car tires. This part of Ishinomaki moved southeast seventeen feet, and down more than two feet. All over the port, water enters and re-enters every wrecked boat, house, and living room.

Slack tide. Road becomes water. The sideways tilt of the houses tells of the Wave's velocity. The ruins are wet; black rain squalls across the open sea. A wind-knife cuts holes. A fisherman, his back to us, pees through a broken door. A dead fish floats by.

When the tide recedes water drains from the new road as if through a boat's scuppers. A single line of cars and trucks bumps over a rickety bridge. Next to it is the collapsed concrete bridge where the Wave drove through.

The seawall that was to protect the town is completely submerged. A tidal ripple crests the top. One young man was trapped on the roof of his house for four days. From there, he could see his mother's dead body floating in the water below.

Rubbish—a two-hundred-foot-high wall of it—lines one side of the road, and on the other side, smashed cars are stacked three high. A paper factory is in ruins, its sawdust piles blowing. A small river is obstructed by a ship turned sideways. Water eddies across its bow and stern.

Trying to get back to the highway, we drive on a potholed road so narrow, we almost go through the front room of another ravaged house. A Buddhist priest walks knee-deep in slush among buildings that have been uprooted like trees. He bows toward a submerged shrine.

This floating world.

At Ishinomaki Where Matsuo Bashō
Once Wrote a Poem

Finally the twisted roadbed drains
and the daily floodtides at
Ishinomaki dry out.
The sky unmists itself and
loss upon loss begins to
feel like company.
Nothing touches. Nights are brittle and soft,
ink scraped smooth.
To the south Fukushima Daiichi blazes. Flames
we can't see. Sixty-six years ago
two other seacoast towns vanished.
I stick my forearm out
in moonlight. Looking seaward
my skin burns.

Ookawa Elementary School

The Ookawa Elementary School was built in the wrong place, set in a narrow floodplain between a wide river held by a levee and an almost vertical forested hill. It's said that after the quake the teachers stood in the playground for twenty minutes and argued about where to take the children. With less than five minutes to spare they made the wrong choice. Seventy-four children and ten of eleven teachers drowned as tsunami waters roared up the Kitakami River and flooded the valley floor. Lives could have been saved if they'd climbed the steep hill directly behind the school, if they had acted quickly. A few did and survived.

Saburo says: "When we were kids, we were self-reliant. The war made us so and the food shortages after. We thought only of how to make our own way and not have to depend on our elders. Now we pamper our children too much. They don't know how to live without being mapped by someone else. That's how it was for these poor schoolkids. Except for a few, they didn't know what to do."

At the bottom of the hill we lay flowers on the makeshift outdoor altar where a black-robed priest bows and prays. On April 28, forty-nine days after the disaster, a ceremony was held for the school's dead and missing. One parent lost her husband and two children. A local fireman lost his daughter and son. A couple attending the ceremony was told that the remains of their child had just been found. They ran from the temple to identify her.

We stare at messages on the altar penned by parents to their missing children: "We are looking for you. We miss you all the time. Please come home."

The levee was meant to protect the school from the river. No one expected the tsunami waves to intrude this far. The narrower the inlet, the more pressure is exerted on incoming water: this wave sped fast upriver and swept away many lives.

The school is windowless, derelict, its floors twisted, the playground deep in mud. Backhoes, front-end loaders, and cranes in the playground stack and remove debris as if to cover the tragedy that occurred here. Palms together, I take a moment to think of the young who died, their teachers, all unsuspecting that this would be their last day of life. I try to comprehend the enormity of this loss, but find I'm only angry. Why would anyone build a school in such a place? Why wouldn't the teachers disobey the evacuation rules and take the children up the steep forested slope in back of the school? The teacher who did climb the hill and survived, later committed suicide.

We pause at the place at the top of the driveway where everyone drowned. It's a mere bump, not even a hill, marked by a single tree. Children clutched the thick trunk but the rushing water was too strong for them.

Kazuko, ever-practical in her superstitions, had refused to go down to the playground and the temporary shrine, and watched from above. She's from rice farmer stock, and like rural people in Miyagi and Iwate prefectures, she believes in ghosts and the divine intervention of the *kamisama*, the gods.

At the car, she pours salt into our hands. "Put it on your shoulders and head," she commands. "To keep the ghosts away. Ghosts don't like salt."

In two months it will be O-Bon, when fires are kindled on mountaintops to welcome the dead. I ask where the dead children are now. "It's a bad thing for children to die before their parents. It's difficult for them now. They are wandering around, waiting."

Water bullies its way into the hearts of things. Its knife cuts loose the coiled lines we use to tie ourselves to what we know. Our familial and spiritual alignments are severed in this "no-stick," unsecured world.

Lost. The river has no shores.

* * *

Kirisame. Soft rain. We're driving west, trying to settle ourselves. We are driving and stopping and walking. Up the emerald green Naruko Gorge we climb, where mountain mist, falling water, and hot-spring steam rises on either side of the car. The sights are balm to our desolation. It's good to be away from the ocean.

Saburo wants to show me a mountain that moved during an earlier earthquake, how it skittered along a fault and toppled. We try to drive to it, but, swallowed by fog, the road to it is closed. Instead, we stop at his aunt's farm. When we slide the outer door open, she's so astonished to see us, she prostrates herself, pressing her head to the floor in greeting, then, sprite-like, pulls out her electric koto to play us a tune.

Those plucked notes from ancient songs stay in my head as we enter a green valley with a river tumbling through. Kazuko hums ancient *jinku* songs as waterfalls cascade down steep cliffs and steam rises. The aesthetic ideal in old Japan was perishability and desolation—*sabireru*. Simplicity led to a sense of beauty measured out in transience and absences, not a machined regularity. To zigzag or make obscure the human passage through gardens was prized; its purpose and essence, however meager, was to suggest, rather than declare. Impermanence ruled aesthetic choices and became an indelible sensibility. On his long walking journeys, though accompanied by friends, Bashō entered loneliness and thrived there.

Below, at the coast, there is no point of view, only town after town scythed by the comings and goings of harbor waves. Up here, the road narrows, and we find Bashō's trail and the obscure paths he trod as a homeless wanderer.

Bashō and his companion, Sora, took a small rice barge downriver; we take a modern road to the town near Mogami and the house where Bashō stayed during a storm. He wrote: "By the time we climbed the big mountain, the sun had already set. Discovering a guard's house, we asked for a place to sleep. For three days a terrible storm raged, and we had no choice but to remain in the mountains." They slept by the horse stalls. His poem:

Fleas, lice—
A horse pisses
Close to my pillow.
 —MATSUO BASHŌ

It's a big-timbered house, low, wide, and dark with twelve-mat and fifteen-mat rooms divided by sliding walls and fading gold-hued murals. The beams are thick and black with age and smoke, but the tatami and thatch are fresh.

The earthen-floor entry has two horse stalls. "I guess he didn't like it here," Saburo says, laughing, referring to the poem. Shoes off, we step up onto tatami. "I like to think he didn't sleep by the horses, that my family was more hospitable to him."

The curator greets us warmly—Saburo is still known here— and stokes the fire in the traditional open pit. He fills a black iron pot with water. After 350 years in Saburo's family, the house was recently donated to the town as a museum. His cousin lives next door.

Tea is served by the curator. Saburo shows me a large round basket where babies are kept, called an *izume*. "I slept in this one when I was a baby and my family came to visit," he says. Smoke from the tea-fire scares insects away. "We always had a fire, even on very hot days," he adds. Lice, fleas, mosquitoes—Bashō mentions them often in his book of travels; I imagine the wonderful sound of horses stomping and eating hay a few feet away.

When the storm subsided that day, Bashō began walking again, first north to Hiraizumi, then southwest into the sacred Dewa Sanzen mountains where *yamabushi* (mountain ascetics), ascetic practitioners, climb ladders of swords, stand naked under freezing waterfalls, and announce the presence of the *kamisama* by blowing on enormous conch shells.

On the way there, Bashō followed a narrow cart track overhung with drooping trees, and stopped to ask a farmer the name of the *michi* on which they were traveling. The old farmer replied: "It has no name. It's just an *oku no hosomichi*—a narrow road to the deep north."

* * *

Sendai again. Exhausted, we eat a quick dinner at a Chinese restaurant—fried tofu with hot sauce, roast pork, spicy chicken, tea and beer—then drive home. Saburo changes his clothes, Kazuko lies on the floor, and Masumi and I take turns in the Japanese-style bath. It's important to scrub our skin and wash our hair to rid ourselves of airborne radiation, though we are told that radiation "passes through" the skin.

Later, Saburo roams the small house in his neatly pressed pajamas. He's lanky and good-natured, and looks healthy enough, but he's been sick since going to a funeral in Kamaishi. The doctors say maybe it's hepatitis A, maybe not, but they've ordered him to stay home and rest, an order he declines to follow.

This house is my temporary home and these three people are

my "family" in a part of Japan where little can be expected in the way of a future, where refugees may be living in temporary housing for a long time, perhaps the rest of their lives. Ephemeral as life may be, we are bound by alternating jolts of unspoken grief and fear of another nuclear explosion. As for the stabbing pain of loss all around us—I can only imagine. Yet from those emotional fissures, from rubbing one's nose in death, a feeling of elation erupts simultaneously.

Mornings and evenings the television is on. We watch the NHK half-hour series about a family, set during World War II. After, the weather news explains each recent earthquake in detail, and since there's a tremor almost every day, there's lots to tell: location of the epicenter, quake depth, duration, crustal deformations, and live scenes filmed from the NHK window in Tokyo as the city rocks and rolls.

Kazuko squeezes into a ball on the floor. She's small, with narrow shoulders and short hair, a rice farmer's thick hands, and a quick sense of humor and delight. Out of the blue, she sits up and says: "Remember Pearl Harbor?" then giggles with her hand over her mouth. Yes indeed, I do, I say, laughing. Why?

Saburo frowns at her. "That's impolite," he quips, but she pays no attention.

"December 7 is my birthday!" she says, exploding in laughter, both hands covering her face.

On the television news we see legions of men in orange, red, or blue uniforms as they continue to search for the missing in Tohoku. Over 28,700 died, and there are still 4,000 whose bodies have not been found.

Early to bed. I lie on my futon with only a sheet over my thighs. It's still so very hot and the air-conditioning has been turned off to save Japan's diminished electricity. I'm rereading a bilingual edition of Bashō's *Narrow Road to the Oku. Oku* means "a depth," the deep interior of the mountains, the inward, wild part of the mind; it is something in one's heart that no one can touch, something well-hidden there.

Saburo told me earlier that people who harbor deep feelings are described as *oku-bukai*. *Oku* also alludes to the word *oku-san*—Japanese for "wife"—because during the time of the samurai, shoguns kept their wives in the back annexes, connected by covered walkways to be sure they were safe. That place was called the *okunoin*.

No matter where we are in the deepest recesses of this house, no one is safe: Fukushima is still leaking radiation.

Night

An aftershock comes in the night, a hard, deep jolt accompanied by the almost inaudible noise of subsidence and mineral grind, as the lesser of the two tectonic plates drives under the other. Masumi cries out, then sleeps again, hypervigilant and exhausted. The quake ebbs and no tsunami siren sounds.

Geophysicists say that space-waves caused by the 9.0 earthquake altered Earth's alignment. I lie on the futon with my feet off to one side, misaligned. Other major earthquakes—the 8.8 quake in Chile and the 2004 quake in Sumatra—have shifted the axis around which Earth's mass is balanced. "Earth is always shifting and wobbling," a geophysicist says. "Nothing stays the same."

Music is time ritualized. From aftershocks, Earth-music erupts: the noise of the crustal rupture under the ocean is a New World symphony whose surfaces seethe with (M_e) of $1.9\pm0.5\times10^{17}$ joules, its crescendo finally released in a series of flaps and lurches, early jolts and mental stresses, and drenching rains.

At the coast the high tide's exuberant wind-waves shatter on rock. There's news of elderly couples committing double suicides. As if to cover the shame of surviving, the ocean reseals itself; its shining surface coheres. Some days I too feel stricken: I can't go back to the coast, I tell myself; I can't look any more. No, that's wrong. I can't *stop* looking.

Dreams wake me: whole forests of the dead roll in at high tide until the mountains of Japan are denuded. I hear the tree trunks' cracking thuds. The real looks unreal. Dreams of disaster cascade through the psyche, as if trying to prop up what has been flattened.

Another mild shake and piano music fattens my ears. A friend of Masumi's says: "In downtown Sendai, we were like dogs on all fours in a big room with twenty grand pianos when the earthquake came. The walls cracked and all the windows broke, and the pianos were rolling around banging each other, making piano sounds. The roof collapsed. We were crawling under pianos in the dark. They were playing the music of seismic chatter."

In a dream I scratch dirt like a dog, panting and frantically working my paws, but the ground is hard-packed and refuses to open. As I travel around Tohoku, I try not to armor myself, but tell me, is there a way to catch grief and tear it open, examine the contents of its stomach? Death stalks us with its internal rain, shed from the same confining canopy that shelters sorrow.

* * *

Morning. Breakfast is being made: coffee, *ocha* (green tea), *gohan* (rice), green salad, and scrambled eggs with a red squiggle of ketchup on top. After the tsunami, a woman who routinely brought farm vegetables to the Yajima house appeared at the door. She apologized that she had only one orange to give. "I was so shocked to see her, I didn't know what to say, so I gave the one orange back and told her to go home. 'You have a child,' I told her. 'We're only adults here. You will need food.' "

Yet the woman returned faithfully each week. There had been an earthquake and a wave and a nuclear meltdown; Tohoku had been ripped apart. "People have to do something," Kazuko explained. One week, cheerful as ever, the young woman bought snacks at the convenience store to give to Kazuko, thinking she had to have something in her hand, because there were no available vegetables at all. The week after, as things in Sendai became more desperate, she came to the door on schedule, empty-handed.

Shoes on, I go out and stand in the middle of the street. There are no cars. An empty lot opposite the Yajima house is alive with tall *susuki* grass waving its blond plumes. Cupping my hands to my ears I hear birds sing and a barking dog moan and go silent. I'm restless and walk the streets back and forth. The noise of this morning's earthquake is the sound of post-disaster Tohoku: stirred sounds rising from embryonic space—lush, chaotic, compressed—yet having no tempo or direction.

What were we not hearing before, during, and after the earthquake? What have we failed to comprehend? I try to pinpoint the event as if that might give me clues, and I prick up my geologic ears, but there's only city noise—cars and trucks on a distant highway, and a siren blaring. Under the epicentral region is the 25,300-foot-deep Japan Trench, where the deepest living fish, *Pseudoliparis amblystomopsis*, is found swimming among mountain ranges with pointed peaks and narrow valleys. So many worlds we don't even see: the airborne one of radiation; the undersea realm of mountains, meadows, and deep valleys lined up like fins on the neck of a dragon. Wave after wave . . .

Some physicists believe that the cosmos is constantly splitting into a multiverse in which quantum objects are broken and unbroken at the same time. As quantum objects interact with the environment, information "leaks away" in a process called "decoherence," and the human is left with a single view. But where does information about the multiverse leak to? In such a world, is a flattened town in Tohoku also unflattened simultaneously? Are the dead also alive?

* * *

On the path that leads back to the house, sunlit spider webs hit my face and burst, and something inside my head opens. Thinking goes *puuuffff*. Boundaries, like seawalls, crumble. A morning moon shines. At the coast, tides do not ebb. Kazuko puts her head out the door and calls me in for breakfast.

Shodo Harada Roshi's Newsletter

In Okayama, far south of the quake's epicenter, Shodo Harada Roshi, the head priest of Sogenji, a Rinzai Buddhist temple, tried to contact affiliated Rinzai temples in Sendai after the disaster, but had no luck. In his newsletter, forwarded to me from a monk in San Francisco, he wrote: "Although we could not communicate directly with them we were able to leave messages." On television the monks were able to glimpse the destruction: "We saw cities burning, we saw a car hanging from a telephone wire, every last thing pushed completely up against a mountain, all fallen over in every direction. We saw people reaching for heavenly help."

Shodo Harada Roshi desperately wanted to help out at Zenoji, where, many times, the abbot there had sent rice and straw sandals to the monks at Sogenji. He wrote: "In any way possible I wanted to go there and support them." The monks worked hard, collecting money in the city, performing *takuhatsu*, an ancient ritual of begging. Loaves of bread were baked—as many as possible before their departure. They gathered candy, cooking oil, shoyu, noodles, chopsticks and bowls, and a kind of gum that cleans the teeth. They brought cases of bottled water and hot packs for children and the elderly, because it was still very cold.

Getting to Sendai took time. The Shinkansen, the bullet train, all local trains, and bus and car traffic had come to a stop. It was not until March 22 that Roshi and two older monks (he did not want to expose younger ones to the radiation) made their way north by car to Kyoto, and by night-bus from there to Sendai.

At Zenoji Temple, the cemetery's sixteen hundred grave-stones had all toppled. Roshi and his two companions helped repair them. As monks, they were allowed to travel on closed roads to help out at other temples. Many Shinto and Buddhist temples within range of the devastated coast became unofficial shelters and temporary morgues. At Furinji, 200 refugees were living on the grounds; at Zuiganji, there were 385 refugees and 16 monks who cooked and cared for them.

It was the invisible that affected Roshi most deeply, the radiation—iodine, cesium-137, and strontium—that was spewing from the Daiichi reactors. In his newsletter he wrote: "Now is the usual time for planting the next rice crop, but it is forbidden by the government. In the whole area radiation has been spreading, in the air, in the things growing there, the vegetables raised there, all of the things nearby are being found to have high levels of radiation. It is impossible not to wonder about this. Today, all over the world, the biggest problem is this . . . the earthquake and tsunami's challenges will be taken care of, but the results of this nuclear power plant will not go away. We can't be deceived by what we see and the circumstances in which we find ourselves. In each and every era we have to see from out of a truly opened eye which is seeing the truth, and not deceive ourselves. This is Zen and this is the harvest of our training."

Three Temples

"Everyone got fat after the tsunami," Masumi's university friend Sachiko says. She's my driver today while Masumi teaches a class, and wheels her tiny car between traffic jams as we search for Zenoji Temple, clutching the steering wheel with fingers so thin, I find them alarming. "At first we didn't have food," she continues. "Then, when we did, we ate a lot."

Sachiko was at Tohoku University when the earthquake hit, standing in a corridor between classes. "I asked a professor what we should do. He said, 'I don't know.' We couldn't think of anything. Books were falling and computers, and all the lights went out. The shaking didn't stop. I thought maybe it would keep shaking, maybe that's how the world would always be."

We find Zenoji in an old Sendai neighborhood lined with rows of bamboo and tiny kitchen gardens jammed against the front doors. The temple's graveyard, with its broken headstones, is imposing. Up the grand stairs, a young priest, the son of the abbot, greets us.

Temples are affiliated and in times of disaster, they help each other in their service to the greater communities around them. The priest remembers when Shodo Harada Roshi and two monks arrived loaded with food to give away. "He wanted to go everywhere, but it was still hard to get around. It was shaking all the time and we were scared, so he helped here, repairing the graveyard, making the wooden sticks—the Toba—and cleaning up the garden.

"We have a thousand people in our *sangha*, our community of practitioners, and only six hundred are accounted for so far. We decided to send postcards with return envelopes. If they were alive, they could send the card back. Only half have done so.

"The roads were still broken but finally we got through to some temples in Ishinomaki, where things were very bad, and eventually got food and clothing to the people who had lost everything there."

The young priest's father, the abbot, appears. Small and white-haired, he sits on the couch facing us. In his presence, the son goes silent. The abbot says: "In our *zazen* practice we try to let go of fear. Whatever happens will happen. We are ready for it. There was another big earthquake the second night Harada Roshi was here so we sat *zazen*. One of the monks—he was a Frenchman—got stuck with his legs crossed. He was so scared, he couldn't move! [*laughter*] Yes, I shall never forget Harada Roshi's visit!"

IKOJI

After making a small offering to help with the refugees, we continue on. Sachiko drives warily on quake-rumpled streets into a maze of ruins, her CD playing "These Are a Few of My Favorite Things." A curved arm of land stretches north from Sendai and holds Matsushima Bay in its embrace.

Wandering among soggy rice fields, we become lost; we back up and try again. At the far end of a narrow track in a secluded valley, we see an upside-down truck, its chassis twisted, lying submerged in mud. Beyond is the entrance to the temple, Ikoji.

The village name, Shichigahama, means "seven beaches,"

though here, there is no view of the sea. Instead, a line of scalloped hills loops across the horizon, a supposed protection from tsunamis.

The temple is low and wide and is situated between the lane and the forest, not on a hill as many temples are. We poke our heads in, looking for the abbot. Instead, the half-rebuilt hall is full of carpenters laying down wide pine planks for the floor. "The abbot is not there, but his wife is in the kindergarten," one of them says.

His wife, Mrs. Watanabe, greets us warmly and invites us into the brightly lit, modern school for young children. Tall and big-boned, she's talkative and funny. She explains that just before the tsunami, a complete renovation of the temple had been completed by master carpenters from Akita, a town on the west coast renowned for its artisans. "It was scheduled to reopen on March 16. But the Wave took it away. Those same carpenters have come back!" she says, smiling at the irony. "We start all over again."

"This temple was supposed to be an evacuation center!" she exclaims. "Can you believe it?" She shows us where water came to the ceiling. "But we always practiced for tsunamis with the three-, four-, and five-year-olds, and thought we were well-prepared, and would be safe.

"No one expected a wave to come here. As soon as the earthquake was over, people from the neighborhood arrived at the temple door. Some ran, some came by car, and the big bell, the *bonsho*, began ringing all by itself!"

A piece of land can be a knife, slicing water in half. "The wave came from two directions," the abbot's wife says. She moves around as she talks, gesturing with her hands dramatically. "The hills on the other side of the rice fields split the water. A wave came in, flowing past the kindergarten and temple. We had fourteen children that day.

"There are two kinds of tsunami warnings and the first one had sounded. Water was everywhere. We put all the children and teachers inside the bus. Then the second warning sounded, meaning another bigger wave was coming, so the staff drove the children up the hill.

"I waited for the woman who had gone back to her house, and sat, ready, in the car. She didn't appear. My husband came running and said he decided that we must go without her. By then about fifty people had joined us.

"At first the car wouldn't start [*laughter*]. Then finally it did, and as I started up the hill, I looked in the rearview mirror and saw the second wave come right toward us. It was big, about seventeen or eighteen meters. It came over the hill and mixed with the water that was already here. It slammed against the fence and went through the temple and the school. Water hit the *bonsho* and it began ringing again. It was really snowing hard. We had closed the doors and windows of the temple, and the heavy shutters, but water and mud made its way in and covered everything. We saw the tatami from the meditation hall floating out in the rice fields.

"We stayed there overnight. The little hill had become an island in a sea of wreckage. Water covered everything below. An oil tank exploded nearby and there was a bright orange light. More explosions and a helicopter flew over, but didn't see us. My husband went back down the hill to forage for food and blankets.

"Inside the kindergarten he found the freezer lying on its side with the door facing up. It was sleeping," she says, getting up to pantomime how her husband opened the freezer. "Meanwhile, a friend of his who had studied with him at Daitokuji got through to some firemen and told them that there were fifty children and adults stranded on the mountain here. Incredibly, rescue workers arrived the next day. It was the children they were worried about. The helicopter hovered overhead and we were hauled up—about ten of us at a time. It took until dark to get us all to safety."

She sits with a thud and a laugh, drained by her own exuberance. Strips of yellow flypaper hang from the ceilings. She sees me looking at them. "Yes," she says, "we are Buddhists, but the abbot says it's okay to kill the flies because, with all the dead around, they could spread disease. We must protect the young from these things."

Children are leaving for the day, being picked up by their mothers. A line of teachers stands outside in the rain holding umbrellas and waving good-bye to their young charges. They bow as the cars pull away.

SHOUNJI

Where the Naruse flows into the Kitakami River we cross a narrow bridge to the east side and follow the river toward a country temple called Shounji. Here, the river makes a wide, sensuous loop, a U-turn that heads north. Small farms and lumber mills line the narrow road. Great white egrets stalk fish in the shallows. Dredges and search boats ply the water: there are still so many missing.

Less than an hour after the 2:46 p.m. earthquake, the tsunami wave surged six miles up the river. People were standing on the levee watching when the water rushed backward. They were taking pictures, while their children were at the Ookawa Elementary School a few miles away. Farmers were working the fields or driving their produce to market. Almost all died.

"A river does not belong to this shore or that . . . it's just a river flowing down," Trungpa Rinpoche, the Tibetan Buddhist teacher, said. The river is the *bardo*. *Bar* means "between"; *do* means "tower," or "island in a river." Together, the words mean "the space between," and refer to every present moment. We could be breathing, or between breaths; we may be treading water between life and death, or tumbling in the dirty surge, gulping salt, to stand on firm ground.

Today the river is wide, flat, blue. The road passes farmhouses with central courtyards, thatched roofs, and large vegetable plots. We stop to ask the way. A tiny, elderly woman emerges from her field with a basket full of green onions and eggplant slung over her arm. She wears the traditional cotton scarf, pantaloons, and rain boots, and her gray hair is pulled back tight. We ask where the temple Shounji might be found. "Up the road," she answers in a soft, measured voice. "But not as far as the one that washed away."

We follow the river road north. Earlier on today's journey, I read a poem by Bashō that used the "cutting word" *ya*, which separates, yet joins, expressions of before and after. It signals something struggling, something coming into being or else leaving what it once was. It is a river word, a word that warns of impending movement, change, and flux, and helps to describe the Buddhist concept of *bardo*.

My friend Tenku Ruff, a Buddhist nun who came to Japan to help survivors, agreed to meet me at Shounji, where another nun, Fukan-san, lives. As we pull up to the temple, Tenku runs down stone steps, black robes flying, to greet me. An American, she speaks Japanese with a soft Florida accent. Her features are sensuous, her face beautiful; her head is shaved. She was ordained in Japan along with Fukan-san, after training at a monastery in Nagoya.

We follow her up the steps to the temple courtyard. An exquisite S-shaped pine tree stands in the center, so old and heavy its bows are supported by vertical sticks—bones braced by crutches. Past the abbot's living quarters, we ascend another set of stairs to the temple. Fukan-san stands at the entrance and bows.

Flickering candles illuminate framed photographs and the vessels that hold the ashes of the recently dead: they are mothers and fathers, farmers and workers, and many children. We bow, light incense, and breathe in their suffering.

Shoes back on, we cross the courtyard to the abbot's living quarters. Shoes off, we step up. In another room the television is on: he's watching the evening news. We're asked to sit and wait. Finally he emerges.

The abbot's entry is quiet. Slender and tall, with a kind face, he sits with impeccable posture. "I have three daughters," he says. "I put them through school, and they haven't been back since!" Laughter. "Then my niece, Fukan-san, came visiting and said she wanted to become a nun. I thought she was joking, so I told her to shave her head. Right then and there. And she did. That meant she was serious, so I sent her to the monastery in Nagoya.

"It takes five very hard years of practice, study, and training to become a Buddhist nun. Fukan-san graduated three days after the tsunami. I was so sorry that I couldn't get there. I'm eighty years old and I need someone to take over the temple. I asked her if she would do it and she said, 'Of course!'" He looks at her with an impish smile. "So I've adopted her as my daughter.

"One of the founding fathers of Soto Zen came from China and that priest's ancestors built this temple 530 years ago. I'm the thirty-second abbot. I hope Fukan-san will be the thirty-third."

The abbot's wife joins us. Green tea is poured. There's a long silence, then he speaks: "No one expected the tsunami wave to come up here on the river. People were standing on the levee watching, not realizing they were in danger. They were swept away, along with most of the children from the school up the road at Ookawa. Many years ago, I went to that same school.

"There were two waves. One was two meters high. It receded and came back as a three-meter wave, a big tsunami wave. The bottom of the river showed. This has never happened before.

The temple up the road, Kannonji, was washed away. It lost all the headstones from the graves. Rice fields were swept clean. No one wants to live in that village now."

He recalls that after the tsunami, it began snowing hard. An eighty-nine-year-old woman showed up at the door. She was soaking wet and shivering. The abbot's wife warmed her and gave her dry clothes. "Earlier, when the earthquake happened, I was only concerned that the statue of the Buddha would fall. Then I realized the tsunami was serious and our whole world had changed. My temple became an unofficial evacuation center and a morgue."

He remembers the Ogachi Bridge collapsing. No one could get out. The commuter train stopped on the tracks and hasn't moved since. "Water came so far in, it was as if the ocean was right here. There was no river, just water stretching across everything," he says, holding his hand to his heart.

Tenku tells of the priest and his wife who went to the second floor of their temple as water approached. "The whole building lifted off its foundations and started floating. It swung near the mountain. They ran out onto the veranda and when the temple floated close enough, they jumped off onto the steep slope and grabbed onto tree branches. From there they watched their beloved temple collapse."

The abbot continues: "After the tsunami water came up this river, we had seventy or eighty people staying here. It's a small country temple and it became too crowded. We had nothing to eat for three days. I sent them to an elderly lady's farm down the road to get some vegetables, and they did, and came back. On the sixth day volunteers came with food and supplies.

One hundred people died who lived near the temple up the road. It's only a roof and a frame now. Then the most extraordinary thing happened: survivors began dragging the dead out of the river and bringing them up the road to us. Some were carried over men's shoulders, others were put in wheelbarrows, or in the back of small trucks. The dead kept arriving. Corpses filled our temple courtyard. They were lying all the way around the center pine tree."

The abbot recalls how the faces of the dead were covered with cuts. The Wave had knocked them around. "They were unlucky," he says. "I felt so sorry for them. Eight adults right here on this little road died, then twelve more were found. Twenty are still missing."

The abbot and Fukan-san took turns performing funeral ceremonies. At the first one, the young nun said there were forty bodies and forty hastily made coffins because the crematorium had been washed away. Just out of monastery, she wasn't sure she could do it. "I opened my mouth and a chant came out. I got to the end without faltering."

When she had to give the dedication and say a few words, she says, "All I could think of to say was, 'Return to the sea.' Later, I called my teacher at the monastery and asked her about it. She told me the words didn't matter as much as the way the heart was speaking."

The abbot: "We had ceremonies here for the dead, even when there were no bodies. Two families in our *sangha* are missing four family members. Only one has been found. But there are still seven missing. Another neighbor never found his family at all. He read in the newspaper that they had died."

The police told the residents to leave the bodies as they found them, as if the river was a crime scene, but the survivors ignored the order and kept searching, and digging, and carrying the dead to Shounji. Funeral services continued. A man who once taught at the Ookawa Elementary School returned to help and still walks the river.

"But the most courageous of them all," the abbot says, "is a young woman who was on pregnancy leave. She had her baby just before the earthquake. But her older daughter, a sixth grader at the Ookawa School, was washed away and hasn't yet been found, so Naomi, the mother, got a license to drive a backhoe. Now she digs for the missing every day. Not only for her own daughter, but for the children of other survivors. So far she hasn't found anyone, but she won't give up," the abbot says, holding his hand against his heart.

The abbot looks tired so we stand to leave. I ask about Kannonji, the temple up the road. He says all that's left of it is the huge bell, the *bonsho*, traditionally hit with a large stick. I suggest they bring it to Shounji and ring it at New Year's to commemorate the dead and those who survived. He says, "Good idea!" His wife agrees. The mood brightens.

The gentle abbot smiles, then frowns: "But if they rebuild Kannonji, we'll have to take it back." I suggest jokingly that they put wheels on it and have the monks push it back and forth. Fukan-san looks at me: "But I'm the only monk!" Laughter. I tell her I'll come and help push. It'll be good Buddhist practice, I say.

* * *

Every instant is death; every instant is birth . . . there's nothing you can grasp onto. The impermanence of the rebirth is the continuity of it.

—TRUNGPA RINPOCHE

* * *

It's what I call "pure bardo." Neuroscientists have named it the "wave of death," referring to a strong wave-shaped signal in the brain that continues after death, after the oxygen supply has been cut off, pressing scientists to ask, When does life end? It represents what Anton Coenen, a science writer, called "the ultimate border between life and death, a massive signature, an eerie shudder of activity that goes beyond the end of breathing."

Night

The surface of the mind trembles without cease,
Like the surface of the waters,
And like the waters
It assumes the shapes of those forces
That press upon it.

—ROBERTO CALASSO

Hard rain begins and crustal instabilities cause the ocean bed to keep moving. Sea foam clobbers city's edge and young waves shoulder Honshu's fractured spine. Two more shakes before dawn, one with a distant tsunami-warning siren. For the very old it must be reminiscent of the Second World War, when Sendai was obliterated and news came of the mysterious A-bomb, twice dropped. In the *Mainichi News,* a woman tells a reporter that she's lost houses twice: once in Nagasaki and again after the tsunami.

Before rain stops, what feels like a mask drops off. Not the face masks we've been wearing to protect ourselves from toxic dust, or the elegant ones I once watched being carved for the Noh Theatre thirty years ago, but the hardened exterior we present to the world, made with a rough skin.

One small boy said, "I feel one way when people are watching, but I'm another person when I'm alone, without my mother or father." Another young boy who watched both his parents drown has not spoken a word since the tsunami.

I sit up in the dark. Too often we do not relate directly to experience. The mask, the scarf around the neck, the tall boots. The mask is brittle. I tear at it and a few pieces fall. Maybe we don't have to take it all the way off, maybe it's enough to let rainwater loosen it, to glimpse the possibility of nakedness. The mask slides, sticks, slides again. I cry for only the second time since coming here. Tears roll and the whole carapace crumbles. It's not so much a question of giving it up; as Trungpa Rinpoche said, "The mask begins to give you up because it has no function for you anymore."

Lying down, my rib cage floats. It rises to the ceiling and hangs there. From it dangle wrists, knuckles, and knees—the bones as light as toys. Rain comes hard and morning light is washed black as if the tsunami's shadow-wave had inked the air and gone back to scrape darkness from stone.

The Van

Don't expect the next moment. Forget this moment
and grow into the next.

—SHUNRYU SUZUKI, ROSHI

The "handover" from Masumi and her family to my new driver
and interpreter took place at Sendai Eki, the huge railway station at city center. Nikki is twenty-six, half New Zealander and
half Japanese. Worldly and bright, she wears a denim wrist-
band with the words: "I ain't gonna be your bitch." The driver,
a forty-eight-year-old long-hair from Kesennuma, has the
unlikely nickname of "Abyss." Perfect, I think, and smile, wondering if the nickname refers to the "abyssal plain" of the Japan
ocean trench, or just the "abyss" of the tsunami.

Kazuko, eyeing Abyss-san's long ponytail, asks me if I'm
going to be all right. I assure her that I'll be fine. She cries as we
drive out of the station.

It's a hippie van with a bed in the back and a solar panel thrown
onto the dash to keep cell phones and MP3 player charged. The
windows are down and music is playing loud. Abyss-san is small
and agile, with thinning hair at the top of his head. Earlier, when
he opened the passenger door for me at the station, he gave me
a half-bow with a knowing smile, then told Nikki she'd have to
sit on the bed in back.

Now he wheels the old van into the throngs of traffic—mostly
policemen and volunteers—with ease. To the south is Fukushima Daiichi, the wounded nuclear power plant still leaking

and steaming, melting and fusing; we head north as it gets dark, up the ravaged coast of Tohoku.

A tropical flush of humidity pushes into stifling summer heat as we weave between small trucks with cranes mounted in back, ambulances, and police cars. The old van holds us in its ramshackle confines. In the back, Nikki makes instant soup with hot water from a thermos and checks emails on her cell phone. Abyss-san says that when he's not volunteering, he makes drums and sells them at a summer festival. To be a hippie in northern Honshu means taking a political stand; he is an outsider and a radical, and unlike so many in Japan, an activist. Nikki, who stands at the fringe of several worlds, sticks her head between us, giving simultaneous translation as Abyss-san tells his stories:

"After the tsunami my mother came to live with me up in the mountains for two months," Abyss-san says. "For forty-eight years I'd caused trouble for her because of the way I live. But after the tsunami, we became close for the first time. Living together was an opportunity to have deep conversations. Then two friends from Kyoto came to help volunteer, and we all lived communally. Once she experienced it, she began to accept me. She liked this way of living. We cooked together, slept in small tatami rooms, used the outhouse, and bathed in the *ofuro,* the wood-fired bathtub. It was more like the way life was when she was a girl."

Patches of blue slide by and are overtaken by radioactive mist. Abyss-san says the government should give everyone a Geiger counter. "The radiation is not just at the coast," he tells me. "It's up in the mountains where I live too. It's everywhere."

Earlier he'd given us a list of dos and don'ts to avoid radiation contamination:

Drink only bottled spring water.
Don't hang washing outside.

Don't use hair conditioners—they hold radiation particles
to the hair, which are absorbed by the scalp.

Cut hair and save it in a Ziploc bag to use as a baseline for
how much more radiation has been absorbed.

Drink 3 grams of charcoal to 3 grams of water a day; eat
brown rice, vegetables, and miso. No meat.

Use coffee filters and charcoal to filter water.

Wash whole body with salt scrub.

In the *ofuro* refill with clean water each time.

For two months after the tsunami, Abyss-san used his van to transport food and supplies to anyone in need. He'd pull up to a center, open the back doors, and say, take whatever you need. He recalls that he got almost no sleep. Friends from distant places showed up and pooled their money to buy toilet paper, diapers, rice, tea, potatoes, cabbage, onions, and carrots for the refugees. "People were hungry," he said. "Some gave what little food they had to their children. I tried to make sure that everyone had something to eat."

His van runs on biodiesel and can also run on propane. When gasoline ran out in every Tohoku town, he could still get around. "If the government had told people about running their cars on propane, some lives could have been saved. The politicians care too much about order and normalcy. That's our Japanese flaw. It does no good to suppress fear and cling to conformity. We have to meet the truth. There is no order now."

Koinobori—cloth fish—flutter from bamboo poles, seemingly taller because everything around them is gone. We drive through Kesennuma, Abyss-san's hometown, where the new baseball stadium, completed just before the *jishin*, is now charred. One lamp pole was left standing, its light twisted and bent around as if peering into someone's ear. The squashed steering wheel of a truck has been pushed to the side and hangs out of the driver's opened door.

A line of blue-uniformed policemen lift the roof of a house that's grounded in deep water to retrieve the dead body of one of the town's hundreds of missing. A few damaged houses have signs that read: "Please don't demolish; there are still important things inside." We pass a "three-up": a house on top of a convenience store on top of a ship. Rubble has been shoved and shaped by bulldozers into a mountain range that mirrors the mountainous spine running north and south through Honshu. "Another version of the Japanese Alps," Abyss-san quips.

As we leave town Abyss-san says, "The tsunami was an incident within prediction boundaries. I knew it would happen someday so I moved from the port of Kesennuma to the mountains in a place with good water. I chose to live this way because I'm not satisfied with the 'normal' world, and as small as I am on the planet, at least I can start being a part of a change. There's so much to be done. I continue to be active in helping now to pay respect to those who died in the tsunami."

A tow truck with a red Ferrari in back zooms by. Nikki flakes out on the bed in back and quickly falls asleep. Three policemen hover over a hole in the ground. We pass a mountain of coal, a dam holding milkshake-brown water, a stone lantern store, a rack of used clothes for sale by the side of the road, an overturned truck, a makeshift used-car lot, a muddy rice field, a boat jammed into a shrine.

A Japanese Rail employee checks the twisted tracks. "During the tsunami whole trains disappeared, buried in mud, passengers still aboard," Abyss-san says. Police cars with lights flashing pass us. It's "rush hour"—a rush away from this painful scene.

Bumper-to-bumper traffic as we pass a house split in three parts atop a damaged overpass, a crushed semi, a tin roof, a bent guardrail dangling. The road is gravel and mud. "The river was the highway the Wave took," Abyss-san says. "All along this coast there were famous beach resorts. Now it's all a 'last resort!' " *Laughter.* "I sometimes wonder if it's worse to survive," he says softly.

I ask Abyss-san if he has a girlfriend and he shakes his head no. "But I'd like one," he says. Down by the ruined port he tries to find the spot where his former house once stood, but he can't figure it out. Except for warehouses, there are no buildings left at all, as if the world had been taken back to a blank slate. "If there are no clues, no reference points, how can I know where I am, if I exist?" he asks.

One last look at the ocean. "Every time the tide goes out, more bodies are found," Abyss-san says. Rain beats hard on the roof of the van. "The radiation is much worse when there's rain," he reminds us. "It carries the airborne particles down to the ground."

A woman in a long black funeral dress, carrying an umbrella, runs on a narrow bank across a rice field.

On the way to Abyss-san's mountain house we stop on a hill. The view of Kesennuma is of a flattened city. "Just after the tsunami I sat here," he says. "Fuel tanks all over the port were exploding. One fishing boat caught fire. Then it got loose from its moorings and drifted. Everything it touched burst into flames. Soon, hundreds of trawlers were burning. It was dark, night, snowing. Fishing boats were pieces of fire floating. They lit the harbor; they were the only lights. The entire world was on fire."

Two Waves

A tsunami wave is born from displacement, not wind, and does not travel over the ocean's surface, but rises suddenly from the rupture zone and drags bottom all the way to shore. As it comes into shallow water, the wave mounds up, and its height increases dramatically. There are stories of fishing boats going out too late and flipping. They faced the Wave and died. None of their crews were seen again. On shore, the Wave plowed through harbors, ports, parking lots, houses, stores, temples, graveyards, and schools. Spilling over bridge railings, it was not a wave, but a black waterfall.

The Wave lifted up and became a mountain. The mountain was water moving, annihilating itself in a crescendo of striated, dissolving foam. I thought it was only one wave, surging and recoiling, but images from the satellite called GRACE recently revealed that "the Wave" was actually a composite.

Two seismically generated wave-fronts merged, deflected from different undersea ridges and troughs. As they moved forward, they came together to form a single wave that, when focused by a narrow harbor, had run-up heights as high as 133 feet.

Radiation News

When news of the tsunami came over the radio, the Greenpeace ship *Rainbow Warrior* turned from direct-action, antiwhaling protests to radiation monitoring off the coast of the Fukushima Daiichi nuclear plant. Their mission is to get at the truth of what has been called by marine biologists the "worst marine radiation contamination in history." TEPCO and the Japanese government have been accused of falsifying numbers and the extent of the marine and airborne radiation pollution during and after the reactors' meltdowns.

"Radiation is a core issue for Greenpeace," Wakao Hanaoka, an oceans campaigner for Greenpeace, says. He's in his thirties, with short-cropped hair and a big belly. His eyes sparkle with enthusiasm as he talks. "We worked on radiation issues in Kamchatka, at the bombing sites. It's one of our strengths."

Many of the local fishermen in the Fukushima area now welcome the Greenpeace campaigners—the very people they've been fighting in southern whaling waters. "They need to know how contaminated the water is, and we help them find out," Wakao-san says. Fishermen are donating samples of seaweed, sea cucumber, oysters, mussels, anchovies, and a variety of fish to Greenpeace, which, in turn, sends the samples to certified nuclear labs in France and Belgium to be analyzed. So far, Wakao-san tells me, fourteen of the twenty-one samples recently sent are over the limit for cesium isotopes and high concentrations of iodine, which indicates liquid discharges from the reactors.

"We need clear guidelines from the government both for the

fishermen and for the consumers. So they know what they're eating and where it came from," Wakao-san says. "We need to study the whole marine ecosystem, the food chain of the fish, the water itself, and the mud and sand at the bottom, because that's where radiation sits."

The entire fishery from thirty to sixty kilometers south of the Fukushima power plant is highly contaminated, including seaweed and oysters. Bottom-feeding fish such as rockfish, flounder, and greenlings have been found to be five thousand times more toxic than they were before the tsunami.

Every morning at dawn, Wakao-san goes to the Tokyo fish market to test for radiation. "They're getting used to seeing me there. When the government tests, they wave a dosimeter over the top of the fish as they come off the boats, but that doesn't work. You have to cut the fish open. I'm getting very good at handling the knife," he says, laughing.

Wakao-san looks for the bright side of the disaster, and sees it as an opportunity for Japanese citizens to become activists. "We must use this chance to raise our voices because the Japanese government no longer ensures our future. For Japanese people the ocean is a factory for seafood. Fish is mostly what we eat. My parents, who are older, think they don't have to be careful, so they eat the *most* contaminated fish in hopes that the less contaminated fish will be there for younger people."

When I ask Wakao-san, who has two young children, if he's still eating fish, he smiles, and says: "I'm Japanese. Maybe not as much, but yes."

Mushiatsui

Morning. Fickle June weather: cloudy, windy, rainy, misty, but mostly hot and humid—*mushiatsui*. In old Japan, weather watchers invoked rainfall by cutting off the head of a swan and throwing it behind a waterfall. In the town of Kuji, near the northern extent of tsunami damage, a swan that lost a wing has been rescued and given a home.

I pick through a pack of Hana Fuda cards, a simple Japanese card game printed on mulberry paper, based on the seasons, and try to see how people here hinge themselves to the natural world: caring for miniaturized alpine rock gardens, growing flowers, living in the play of light and shadow through paper doors.

Pine bough, flower, insect, bird, *o-sake*, and *o-mizu* are the shuffled emblems of seasonal shifts and transience, of luck, life, plentitude, and perishability. June's card features "Peony (for beauty and medicine) with Butterfly (for transience and change)."

We take a torturous coast road that is tree-shrouded and buckled when it exists at all. The ocean view is intermittent because of the trees. The scenes below, when we can see them, resemble a painting by Hieronymus Bosch: you can count the dead and missing; you can see how a hill functioned as a knife slicing oncoming water; you can step through what's left after the Wave. In one place, a Mitsubishi F-2 fighter jet banged into a damaged building. The steel ribs of a fish factory are bent over shredded rubble that resembles combed hair. Nikki gets a Tweet about the Red Sox pitcher Daisuke Matsuzaka, who donated a million dollars to Tohoku's disaster relief fund.

Losing altitude, we pass through the remains of towns and villages. Half of the town of Otsuchi was flattened, its marine research lab destroyed. It's here that Dall's porpoises are slaughtered for food. Members of the Sea Shepherd Conservation Society have tried to stop the capture and killing of these cetaceans, but since being caught in the tsunami, they've become volunteers, helping other survivors.

Miyako

The ocean is roaring. Waves are stacked and sucking in whatever had seemed permanent, throwing it forward again like an uncaught ball. Old men, teenagers, children walk the roads, sit on seawalls, crouch on broken tree trunks in the shade, stunned by summer heat and disbelief, stilled by grief. Seawalls were built in front of these big northern coastal fishing towns at the expense of an ocean view. "How strange to live on the ocean and not see it," Abyss-san says. "And then have the thing that blocks the view turn out to be ineffectual."

The seawall in Miyako, one of the large northern fishing ports affected by the tsunami, failed completely. Firemen tried to close the massive steel water gates by hand as the wave topped the seawall. Metal was bent like tinfoil. Water broke through, and the firemen were swept away.

At the main port we see only a few boats. Any fisherman close enough to the harbor jumped on his boat and went out full throttle toward the wall of water that advanced toward them. "Every boat you see on the water now is one that was saved by its captain," a worker in the temporary harbormaster's office tells us. He offers us the use of the fishing co-op's rubber boots, and says we are welcome to wander around.

He shows us where the wave washed over the tops of the warehouses, and is proud of the rebuilding they have accomplished already. Luckily, they had recently stored hundreds of tons of ice farther inland so they would have enough for the hot summer season. "All the ice factories were destroyed up and down the coast. But because we have this reserve, we're open for business today. We had one of the biggest waves here because of the shape of the harbor. We lost most of our 950 trawlers. But if you want to talk to someone who got his boat out in time, wait here. He's coming in today."

A fifty-foot trawler slides up to the loading dock, manned by a father-son team, its entire aft deck stacked with plastic baskets of giant Pacific octopus, throbbing and writhing, confined and confused. They are the smartest of all invertebrates, and their half-billion neurons must be firing now. What did they know of the earthquake? How did their behavior change? What are they thinking now?

"Like the rest of us, they have one thing only on their minds: escape," Abyss-san quips. When the bins have been unloaded and taken under the roof of what was once the fish factory to be iced, the father leans over the rail and offers his story.

"When the quake came I knew there would be a tsunami so I drove to the harbor, got on my boat, pulled anchor, and started out. My boat is about fifty feet long. Suddenly it lifted up into the air. It was the wave coming in. It felt as if we were being lifted up from beneath—we were eighty meters up above the bottom of the ocean, and stayed there for about three minutes.

"The water was rough and confused, moving every which way. It was hard to steer. I kept going. Another ten minutes out I thought I'd be safe. There's a little island out there. I thought it would be far enough. Then I saw the horizon was all white again. This was the big wave coming. It came in fast and submerged the island's lighthouse. It came under my boat and lifted it 120 meters above the ocean bottom, and still, I could see more waves coming. I turned and looked: waves were crashing over the seawall, through the harbor, pouring through town.

"I stayed out for two days. I was afraid to come back in. There were about ten boats out there. No one had any warm clothes, much less water or food.

"I was cold and hungry. The water was moving in strange ways and it was covered with debris. My house was at the foot of the mountain. I looked with binoculars trying to find it. Only the roof was left. I saw the house poles being carried away by small waves. I couldn't call my wife. Our cell phones didn't work; there was no reception. But another fisherman came alongside and told me the entire coast had been destroyed.

"It was snowing. A navy ship came by and gave us emergency food—water and a few biscuits. When I finally went back in, there was no harbor. It was hard to find a place to tie up the boat. After finding a secure mooring, I walked up above town and found my wife. She was fine. We know about tsunamis here. We know to go to high ground."

His family was taken to an evacuation center and has been there for three months. "At first we hardly had any food. They gave us one rice ball and one liter of water a day for the first twenty days! My wife lost a lot of weight. It was a good diet!" he says, laughing.

"Now temporary housing is completed and we move in this weekend. I didn't want to stay in the communal center. It's better being with our neighbors rather than outsiders—people from other towns. Here, we are all fishermen and we understand and worry about each other."

Blue bins of octopus are stacked by female fish market workers in blue aprons and rubber pants and boots. Suddenly the dock and the boat begin to rock. The father stops talking and a terrified look comes over his face. The boat pulls at its mooring lines.

The women are vigilant, waiting for the shaking to stop. The fisherman peers over the rail at the water: "I felt a bit of a shake. Maybe I'm paranoid now. Since the tsunami, I'm always getting ready to go back out. The ocean is different now. It looks and moves in a strange way. There can always be another tsunami."

Before March 11 there were three strong earthquakes and the fishermen and their families who live close to the water were evacuated each time. The father says he had noticed signs of something different for two or three months before. The tide started coming from north to south, and it moved faster than usual. It had done that the year before too.

"But the March 11 earthquake was outsized. Now the bottom of the ocean is filled with houses and cars. We'll never be able to go back to normal ways of trolling." He shakes his head, gives a slight shrug, and signals to his son that it's time to go. Stepping up to the bridge, he revs the engines.

"We're still fishing, though," he yells over the roar. "We went out one month after the quake. In December, the catch is crabs; from April on, it's all *tako*—octopus. You should talk to my son," he says, looking over his shoulder proudly at the tall young man whom he calls Masayuki. "He's got his own boat, and he writes a blog. You can read it every day."

The young man says nothing, but smiles shyly. He secures the lines with an agile ease. Maybe if you have seen seawater rush back, baring the ocean floor, then return to take everything you know, you've seen the world.

Three women untie the mooring lines and flip the thick ropes to Masayuki. He catches and coils them on the deck as the trawler slides away.

Hirayama Masayuki:
The Idle Blog of a Fisherman

http://blog.goo.ne.jp/heiun

March 9

Just had an earthquake as we were heading home after unloading our catch. My truck started shaking the moment I got in. I thought at first the wind was shaking it. If a tsunami comes . . . We went back out anyway and waited for the emergency tsunami warning to be cleared. We could see no changes, so we sailed back to port, but there was a vortex on the wave surface as we came in . . . Whoaaaa . . . A rare sight.

March 10

We're going out to check the floating equipment. There's a chance that some of it got washed away or a chance that a load of crabs have scuttled into our cages! If the waves get rough, it might be a difficult journey home . . .

We plan to go out tomorrow too, but I wonder what's going to happen. It seems there have been a lot of earthquakes today, not to mention the one yesterday, a 7.2.

March 11

3:00 p.m.: A huge earthquake has hit. Getting the boat out as fast as we can and heading toward the ocean.

3:04 p.m.: The tide is pulling out fast at Miyako Port. This is the biggest earthquake ever.

3:09 p.m.: We're going at maximum speed out to the ocean. Here comes the tsunami.

3:20 p.m.: The tsunami is coming toward Heizaki! Oh my god! . . .

3:23 p.m.: The waves are pushing at the cliffs. They're really high.

3:26 p.m.: Tsunami approaching Sakiyama to Anegasaki.

3:44 p.m.: Big trouble in Miyako Port. According to the radio, the port is flooded and stuff is washing out everywhere. I can see smoke, maybe fire? Power has gone out on land.

March 12

4:56 p.m.: Kuwagasaki (where we live on the north end of Miyako Port) is destroyed.

March 14

I couldn't bring anything with me as I had to rush out with my boat as soon as the earthquake hit. There just wasn't time. No time even to think if I wanted to save my own life, to escape. Because I have no food, the hunger is hitting me hard. The other boats are in the same situation. We saw a Navy vessel in the north. I heard on the radio they are distributing food, so we are going toward them.

They have given us two rice balls, a tin of mackerel, a bottle of tea, and a packet of cookies. Now we're saved. I thanked them over and over again. They seemed like gods to me.

March 18

The shock of losing my house, losing everything is immeasurable. Beyond shock. I have no tears. The old lady living next door in the B&B was washed away, and the grandmother across the street from us is also missing.

March 19

This morning we received a rice ball, miso soup, and mineral water. The hotel where we have been evacuated gives us three meals a day. Mainly rice balls and water. But to eat food is simply wonderful.

March 22

After breakfast I went to the shore. We tried to clean around the fishing warehouse. There were boats and nets and buoys and clothes swept away to unbelievable places. There's a ridiculous amount of theft going on here. They're coming in from out of town and looting. Security is zero. The safety of our small town has been destroyed.

March 28

The tsunami collapsed the main bridge. There have been more suicides. It's irresponsible to say "*ganbatte*"—"do your best." If anything, it has the opposite effect.

March 30

I have to go to a lot of temporary offices to do my paperwork. I'm not at the evacuation center much. I grab my food and go out and come home before evening. This is what we had tonight: one rice ball, two slices of apple, and a bottle of juice. This is our usual evening meal. Early start tomorrow so going to bed. I'm worried about our nutrition, but can't complain. Good night.

North Miyako Bay

To the north of the main harbor—what's left of it—three older fishermen are repairing their skiffs. One man leans against the bow of his small boat as we approach. "I need to get back out quickly," he says after sizing us up and deciding he'll talk to us. "I have only this small boat, so I catch only small fish—sea urchins and shellfish, mostly. My skiff was washed ashore and I found it. There was a big hole in the hull. Now I've fixed it. The government is busy. There's no use waiting for them. We're fixing things up as best we can.

"We've been told to move to higher ground, but we're men of the sea and you can't tell us to grow vegetables. We have traditions and techniques that have been passed on to us, and we can't change over to farming just like that.

"I saw the tsunami and still, I'm not afraid. We're just like animals. It's our instinct to survive. Not because of fear, but just because that's what we know to do. Most of us around here believe we must live on the ocean. We can't live in a city apartment. It isn't fun to live without facing challenges. I've faced death three or four times already. That's why I'm not afraid now. Or maybe I'm just stupid!" He laughs, lights another cigarette, and keeps talking.

"When I'm out on the ocean, there's only this one piece of wood that separates me from death." He touches the bow of his boat and gazes at it affectionately. "As soon as the quake hit I watched the birds. They all flew away. The announcements on the loudspeakers mean nothing. I always watch the birds. They told me to run. I was here at the waterfront when the Wave came in. I saw the tide push back and the seaweed twist on the ground, so I tied up my boat and hurried up the hill. People who forget Nature, forget how it works, they are doomed.

"I've been fishing since birth. I catch whatever is out there and sell it at the market alongside the big boats. We need only to live according to our instincts and needs. My boat's name is *Honfukumaru*—'*A long breath of Wind.*'"

* * *

Die while you live.
Be utterly dead.
Then do as you please.
All is good.
—SHIDO MUNAN

On the Road Again

We're on the road again and Abyss-san plays that song. I roll down the window. What I thought would be fresh air is instead full of the stink of decadent refuse. Nikki sits cross-legged on the plywood platform in back, translating when she has to, checking emails and Tweets when she doesn't. When the road straightens out, she gives a rough translation of a piece written by a Japanese journalist, Shin'ya Hagio, who is dedicating a year to collecting stories from Tohoku for his newspaper, the *Mainichi News*. He writes:

"Not far from here a father and his two sons were found living in the hills in a tiny hut built from scraps: a piece of boat is the living room, and it's lashed under a makeshift roof made of building scraps. A long house beam juts out and is covered with tin roofing to make a veranda. The family survives on canned goods found in the rubble. They have only the clothes they were wearing when the wave came. On washdays they melt snow for wash water and stand naked, waiting for the sun to dry their clothes. (Why they live this way is puzzling. They could have gone into town and joined the other refugees in an evacuation center.) The father said only that he can't face people right now. He'd watched his wife, his pregnant daughter, her four-year-old, a second daughter, and his own mother drown.

"The boys walk to a school up on the hill. Now the classes are mixed with people from nearby towns. The older boy plays baseball and likes it. His position is shortstop. But his younger brother has refused to play since he lost his glove in the tsunami. He only says this: 'I miss my mother's cooking.' "

Down from the mountains we come to the town of Kamaishi. Our way is blocked by a ship that has come on shore. The *Asia Symphony* is not a musical group, but a 4,724-ton cargo ship pushed by the Wave into the middle of what was once a busy street. Its red bow sliced through a concrete wall until it rested on the white dividing line. At one hundred meters in length, it's too massive to move until the rest of the debris is taken out of the harbor. We follow the bicycles and cars that pass around it as if it were just another building in the way.

High on a hill a huge white statue of Kannon looks down on Kamaishi's ruined harbor. What does the Goddess of Compassion think now? I ask Abyss-san. He smiles. "She says she has a lot of work to do." Laughter. We're looking for an eighty-four-year-old geisha whose life was saved by a sake merchant who hoisted her on his back and ran to safety. She's been dubbed "The Last Geisha of Kamaishi," and we find her in an evacuation center, once the gym of a junior high school.

Her dancing name was Chikano Fujima, though she's also known as Tsuyako, or "Ito-san." Still a beauty, with high cheekbones, gray hair pulled back tight, and sparkling dark eyes, she is the last holder of an ancient song, an *uta* called the "Hamauta," or the "Kamaishi Bay Fisherman's Song."

"People wanted to hear it again," she told me. "And I'm not going to let the tsunami get in the way." She had been preparing for a summer performance when the tsunami came.

"The Hamauta always brought fish into the nets; it brought prosperity. I used a basket as a prop and put fish into it. There was a special Kamaishi dance that went with the song. When I performed it, everyone was quiet. I'm the last person alive who knows the song."

Now her house is gone but the restaurant where she worked as a geisha still stands. The Saiwai Rou is beautiful inside, but after the tsunami it became a soup kitchen: the owners housed and fed two hundred people. These days it's a restaurant again, and townspeople are holding their funeral dinners there. "Of its one hundred twenty years of operation, I was there for seventy of them," the geisha says proudly.

Ito-san was fourteen when she left school and went to the Shibashi area of Tokyo for training to be a geisha. "It's what I always wanted to do. I'd go and see their performances and feel a passion about it: I wanted to be just like them." She skipped school and instead learned to play the shamisen. "I was told I had a good ear. I loved it. I've always performed, even now. At least, before the tsunami.

"When I was young the ironworks in this town were big and there were lots of fishermen here too. The fish market was very active. Whenever there was a storm, the fishermen tied their boats together and came into the bars and I'd play the shamisen and entertain them. There were many geishas then. Now I'm the last one."

She lived upstairs at the restaurant and performed downstairs at night. During the war Kamaishi's iron factories were targets and she had to flee. In another town she married a sushi chef and had one child. "It was not the life for me," she says, "so I left when the war ended and came back here." Later, she moved in with the head of the geisha training school. "His wife had left him, so I took his name and his tradition."

Ito-san's eyes light up when I point to the photograph of her that graced the front page of the *New York Times* as well as the *Mainichi News*. It's pinned to a cardboard box next to her futon with a wooden clothespin. Since then, she's had a constant stream of visitors, much to the amusement of the other refugees. She's a country geisha, not a slim, polished, white-faced performer from Kyoto, but she has a vivacity that they don't have. More often than not, her determined mouth is set in a beautiful smile.

Ito-san takes my hand and tells me her most recent news: someone found her obi in the rubble and returned it to her, though everything else in her house was lost.

"Where's the man who saved your life?" I ask. "I'd like to meet him." She smiles, stands, and says, "Let's go find him." Abyss-san pulls the van to the front door and, despite his attempts to assist her, she jumps into the high front seat with a young woman's agility.

Down the ruined streets we go, past the huge ship and its red hull, looping up the hill past the restaurant where Ito-san performed, and around again. Her window is open and she waves at everyone like a queen. People run to the side of the van to greet her. "You are looking wonderful," they say.

She points to the remains of a large two-story structure on a corner. "That's my house," she says excitedly, and doesn't seem to mind that it's in ruins. "I was trying to get to the front door during the earthquake but it was shaking so hard, I couldn't stand up. That's when Hiroyuki Maruki, my friend who sells sake, came by. When he saw me crawling, he stopped. Then he just reached down and pulled me onto his back and started running. He carried me all the way up the hill, just as the tsunami water began coming in. He saved my life."

We stop the van in front of what was the local liquor store, now emptied. She asks her friends where Hiroyuki-san might be. They tell her he's living in temporary housing right next to the evacuation center where she and her nephew are camped. "He's still taking orders and delivering sake too!" they say. When we get back, he's waiting for us. They'd called him and told him we were on the way.

"Oh, she was heavy," Hiroyuki-san says, laughing. "I carried her up this hill over there," he says, pointing. "We spent the night there; we watched our houses wash away. But I saved the family dog. He's not as heavy!" And out from under his arm comes a small white poodle.

The next day the survivors were told to go to a temple. But when they got there, they found it was burning down. They were then directed to go to the school gym. Well-known and loved by all, Ito-san was taken care of quickly. Hiroyuki-san says, "They found a special futon for her and she's been on it ever since, receiving visitors from all over the world. Al Jazeera is coming tomorrow!"

Ito-san looks at Hiroyuki-san with pleasure. "I've known him since before he was born," she says excitedly. "I'm the seventh generation in my family in the entertainment business. It may end up with me. I'm not sure if I'm going to set up shop again. My children live in Chiba Province. They've invited me to move in with them. But"—she gives Hiroyuki-san a hug—"I'd rather stay here with my friends."

Boxes surround her futon. Her nephew, Satoshi, an architect, resides in the cubicle next to hers. He watches the procession of visitors with a look of respect and amusement, referring to his aunt as *sensei*—teacher.

Someone kneels beside me. Ito-san looks up, puzzled, then I look too: it's a young geisha in full regalia, but this one is Caucasian, not Japanese. "You are beautiful," Ito-san says.

Her name is Sayuki. Heavy-set with a smooth face, her mannerisms are correct and formal, though she's Australian. "I'm a western Geisha," she tells me and says she wears dark contacts to cover her blue eyes. It's her third year performing in Asakusa, an entertainment area of Tokyo. It was there that she heard about Ito-san. "People in the geisha world were worried about her; that's why I've come north today." She hands a carefully wrapped package to Ito-san. It's a kimono. "To take the place of the ones you lost," she says.

When the Australian geisha and her driver stand to leave,

Hiroyuki-san gives me something in a paper bag: a lovely bottle of sake. "You see, I'm still in business, even if I have no store! I make deliveries. If you like sake, please accept this. And thank you for coming from so far away to meet us," he says.

Ito-san's eyes sparkle. She leans in close and whispers: "Would you like to hear something?" I bow and nod yes. Out comes the shamisen from under a soft cloth. Hiroyuki sits on his heels attentively. As Ito-san tunes her instrument, he whispers, "I love this song. It pulls at the heart."

Slowly Ito-san begins plucking the three strings. Her voice quavers at first, then grows stronger, and the words of the Hamauta begin.

Two gifts: the bottle of sake, and the hum of the cavernous room going quiet as it fills with the sound of Ito-san's sweet song.

All Sentient Beings

Thousands were evacuated from the area around Fukushima Daiichi but no one counted the animals left behind. Farmers, horse breeders, pig and chicken farmers, and owners of pets were forced to flee. Some were told they would be gone for only one night, so they left food and water behind for the animals. But they were not allowed to come back. Dogs left tied up died of dehydration and starvation. Others, unchained, succumbed to infections caused by cuts after being tossed around by the tsunami. Dairy cows died with their heads in stanchions; horses left in stalls were battered by the earthquake and couldn't get out. They ended up starving to death. Many small animals drowned.

All sentient beings. Not just humans. Everything that lives and breathes, plus the inanimate and the spirits floating around Japan—all are equally important. Elizabeth Oliver, the founder of Animal Refuge Kansai—known as ARK—together with the Tokyo bureau chief of the *Economist,* Henry Tricks, were some of the first people to rescue animals inside Fukushima's twenty-kilometer zone. "We know that many people died," Elizabeth said, "but the animals didn't even have a chance to run for their lives."

Veterinarians sprayed lime over the dead livestock to prevent the spread of disease. One dairy farmer refused to leave his animals behind and stayed to care for his cows. A man with 330 beef cows could not bear to abandon them, despite the fact that they no longer had any dollar value. He is permitted to enter the zone to feed the cattle, and gives out extra hay and grain for the strays that come streaming in. No one will ever know how many animals have died or how many still remain.

Elizabeth and Henry recall arriving at a stable still full of horses. Henry said, "Rushes and driftwood tangled up in the halters hanging on the wall suggest the tsunami rose high up above the horses' necks. Some of the stalls collapsed under the weight of the water. In the sun outside, six of the horses lay dead. Many of the living were lacerated along their legs and necks, suggesting sheer panic as they tried to climb out of their stalls. Remarkably, many survived. Their big trusting eyes conceal unimaginable suffering. Their emaciated bodies say more."

Elizabeth said that some of the horses could not walk up the loading ramps: "They had to stay behind, which broke our hearts."

Elizabeth is a British citizen who came to Japan by accident. Waylaid on a round-the-world trip three decades ago, she never finished her journey. Twenty years ago she founded ARK with a group of volunteers and friends and has established two animal rescue shelters, one in Tokyo and the other in Osaka, and is building a large facility in Sasayama, her home in the mountains near Nara.

Since the tsunami, she has been sending frequent newsletters. The most alarming of them announced that the government was intending to ban people from entering the twenty-kilometer zone after April 22. Anyone caught inside was to be given thirty days in jail and fined 100,000 yen. On May 12, the government decided to slaughter all livestock in the zone.

Horses have been bred in Fukushima Prefecture for over a thousand years and their annual Samurai and Horse Festival is famous. A Japanese horse rescue group, Hisaiba, was contacted by ARK and arrived a week later to transport animals to their shelter just outside the thirty-kilometer zone. "When we arrived there, the horses' eyes lit up as they seemed to come alive know-ing they would be safe," the head of Hisaiba said. Two hun-dred Fukushima horses in the no/go zone were adopted by the wealthy Hokkaido racehorse breeder, Katsumi Yoshida, who shipped them by truck and ferry to his sixteen-hundred-hectare farm.

As word spread about the animals around Fukushima Daiichi and the ones lost on the Tohoku coast, animal rescuers began penetrating the no/go zone.

Mayu was wearing three-inch wedge tennis shoes, heavy makeup, jewelry, and tight jeans when I met her inside a crowded Tokyo donut shop. She had never rescued an animal before the disaster, and doesn't own a pet. Now she's one of the guerrilla animal rescuers.

"A friend from Fukushima City called and asked if I would go to the thirty-kilometer zone to look for animals that had been left behind," she began. "I said yes. We found dogs tied up and left to guard the houses. They were hungry. We poured out piles of dog food for them and brought water.

"It's impossible to tell where the thirty-kilometer zone ends and the twenty-kilometer zone begins. We just kept going fur-ther in. When we got to the fifteen-kilometer zone there were signs left by the police that said, 'Please don't enter. Danger Zone.' We kept going.

"The towns were completely vacant. So many dogs roaming around with collars on. The dogs that weren't tied up came to us. We fed and watered them and put them into the car. None of them tried to bite us. They knew we were there to help. We had a four-wheel drive with cages in the back. We went looking for the ones left inside. It was weird breaking into people's houses. But we got a lot of dogs out and drove them the three hours to the shelter in Fukushima City.

"That's how our days were: we'd arrive by nine or ten in the morning and leave by four. There were some police who saw us. They warned us that if we were killed by wandering thieves, no one would find us. But most of the police felt sad for the animals and encouraged us. They just said, 'Be careful, and good luck.'

"It was impossible for us to rescue cattle and horses. We only had a car. But we saw some and they were in bad shape. We went to a town that had been flattened by the tsunami and saw dead horses. All I remember is the horrible look of starvation on their faces. Their eyes had fallen out, and they were lying on their sides.

"At some point it became illegal to enter the inner zones. Barriers were erected and we couldn't get the car through. The government said they were going to euthanize all the animals left behind, despite the fact that some of us were willing to go in and get animals out. I heard that the police were 'euthanizing' cows by rubbing detergent down the cows' throats, leaving them convulsing. A group of us sent a plea to use real medicine. After the lockdown on the zones, we still tried to get it, but they stopped us.

"This was my first time at animal rescue. I spent a total of thirty days inside the no/go zones. I don't worry about radiation. I'm twenty-seven and live in Tokyo. I have no children. We were probably exposed to much more than we knew about at the time, but it doesn't worry me. I feel I did the right thing.

"The dogs I rescued remember me. I can't have a dog where I live, but I've 'adopted' a little white dog that is at my friend's shelter called SORA. She waits for me to come."

North of Fukushima Prefecture, on the Tohoku coast, dogs ran during the earthquake or were washed away by the tsunami. A group of rescuers from a sanctuary called Dogwood outside of Sendai began looking for animals.

The founder said, "After March 11, the police weren't letting us in. I was trying to get to the places covered with water— to Ishinomaki, Higashi-Matsushima, and Natori, but when we finally got to the coast, there weren't any dogs around. Most of them had drowned in the Wave.

"A little further inland we found dogs inside cars, using them as a house. A call came from a woman whose dog had survived the Wave, but had heart problems. She wasn't allowed to bring the dog into the evacuation center, so she was living with it outside in a tool shed. When we located her, she and the dog were shivering; it was snowing hard.

"So many owners have never had the experience of being separated from their dogs. We offered help: we said we'd keep the dogs safe and warm and well-cared for until they were more settled. But when these people went into temporary housing, they found the spaces so small it wasn't possible to keep the dog, so we are keeping them even longer.

"There are 150 dogs here right now. Some are unstable and others don't change despite all they've experienced. They can cope with it. We find that the unstable dogs are mirroring the owners' fears. The strong dogs know to wait; they know some-one will come for them again. If the dogs are happy and ener-getic, then when the owners come to visit—even if they are still unable to bring their dogs home—they feel better too. The dogs influence the humans and vice versa.

"The dogs we received from the twenty-kilometer zone around Fukushima have owners but have not been reunited. We're not sure where the owners are. We've made a book of photographs of the dogs that get posted online to help own-ers and their animals meet up, just as they did with the human survivors.

"We didn't enter the no–go zone, but some dog lovers have been sneaking in and bringing dogs out. Those animals are checked for radiation and if they have high counts, we wash them very thoroughly and have the vets check them. They are all okay. We will keep them for as long as is necessary. They're happy here. And so am I. Compared to those who lost houses and loved ones, I'm very lucky. There's lots of work here but it's good to be able to help."

Abyss-san's Mountain Home

Past verdant pastures of dairy cows and hillside apple orchards, we follow a steep road so narrow, the blue hydrangeas on the road brush both sides of the van. Flowers and vegetables are planted in highway medians. Onions and cabbages reach the front steps of country houses. "We don't have much land, but what we have is well used," Abyss-san says. The intense heat is exhausting, and winding up the steep mountain with opened windows, the breeze grows cooler with each mile.

Abyss-san's mountain house is spare and traditional—tatami rooms with sliding doors between, and a small kitchen down one step. No indoor plumbing except one faucet in the kitchen—just a "long drop" as Nikki calls it, an outhouse—no heated toilet, no bath, no air conditioner.

The night is cool. Mist spews out from between towering cedar trees. The house is a comfortable mess stacked with Abyss-san's unsold drums and boxes of donated goods for refugees that he has not yet delivered. Quietly, he goes to work in the kitchen, making a hearty soup of lentils, cabbage, and carrots on the one-burner gas flame. We each drink a beer.

I go for a walk up the road. Beyond his house there are no neighbors. A line of trees meets small clearings. A hayfield is lit by the moon; the moon is erased by wafting mist. A V of trees, like a widow's peak, divides the road and cuts a vertical slash in the clouds to reveal stars.

Japan has always had itinerant poets and painters, some in political exile, some just sauntering to "cut through attachment." Now the country is full of internal refugees. As I wander back to the house, low clouds brush treetops, and a line from one of Su Shi's poems written in exile comes to mind: "Drifting clouds—so the world shifts."

Abyss-san stirs soup to music—a Japanese-style country song based on Don McLean's lines: "This will this be the day that I die." Abyss-san muses: "We have to adapt back to a simpler way of living," and pours coffee beans into a hand-cranked wooden grinder. Nikki cuts a large apple into three pieces to be shared.

"If food, housing, and job shortages last a long time, things will have to change," Abyss-san says. "Maybe it will bring us back to the old ways, the traditional Japanese style of farming, eating, bathing, living on tatami. And if it weren't for the nuclear radiation, we could all be growing our own food."

In the morning Nikki and Abyss-san sleep, and I saunter again, this time going the other way, up a steep hill. Such a pleasure to be alone in the cool mountains. A Japanese bush warbler sings loudly. They are small and greenish brown but their voices are loud. I come on a huge stone *tori'i*—a gate that opens the way to a mountain path straight up the hill. I climb mossy stairs. Here and there are stone lanterns, gravestones, a piece of rock on a pedestal shaped like a penis.

Cedar trees, a hundred feet tall, crowd the path, their branches laying filigreed shadows on moss. Thick trunks strobe sunlight. Is the temple up top a place to pray for fertility and renewal? I think of the seventeen miles of mountain stairs I climbed on the sacred mountain of Omei-shan in western China. This is just a steep hill. Why is one mountain sacred and the other secular? Far below, at the coast, is a world of lost lives, illegible debris, and sorrow. Will this disaster show the way to more aware lives?

I stumble, then something takes me up and up, my legs turned by tree-spokes, my body pulled by shadow shafts, as if harnessed to something—maybe what I've seen below. Yet the freight is hollow-boned and light. I trot and grin. We think we have time to love, cook dinner, take walks, become enlightened, but one wave can take us, or it can spit us out. Bruised and drenched, we find we are still alive, and the great power of the thing, the megathrust or the Level 7 meltdown that alters time and shakes the planet on its axis, polluting it, feels true enough.

My mind keeps trotting. I turn thoughts loose like horses. Sun-sparks strike my cheek. Mist lolls between branches that huff green oxygen. Radioactive dew shines. My breath mixes with the gasp of trees.

Shunyata

At a convenience store where we've stopped for iced coffee, Nikki teaches me two *kanji* for the word *empty*. I'm looking for coffee with no sugar, and the Chinese character for "nothing," or "not there," *kara*, meaning, "without sugar" (and also "sky"), is marked on the can. Another word for "nothing" is *mu*, a Buddhist word that can imply "not one, not nothing, not no, not yes," and also "the emptiness from which compassion arises."

The character for *mu* "empty" is written as a square-ish grid with four "tassels" on the bottom. These refer anciently to a tasseled dancer performing in front of the gods, during which it is forbidden to show any ties with the human world, and is therefore pure *mu*. Egoless. Unbiased. Open.

I find the coffee, coffee without empty calories, coffee without the ornament of sugar. I do not want to put "things" or projections between myself and experience, though I often do. I sometimes sugar my perceptions or make them bitter, but what I aim for is something more straightforward.

It's said that if we can drop the bothersome appendages of egos and sugar lumps, we will begin to feel an immense caring for others, for otherness, for all kinds of suffering, and in doing so, we will be able to exchange ourselves for others. If we try, strange sympathies will fill us and the power of empathy will fuel us forward.

Four children run out of a broken house and blow bubbles through a plastic hoop. They float for a moment, then burst. Is that how children come to understand impermanence? Their mother picks through a box of scavenged goods, through whatever remains: water-stained papers, a single shoe, a lacquer rice paddle. Flies cover a photograph of two schoolchildren, and as the day heats up, insects increase in number.

When I arrived in early June we wore white face masks when visiting the coastal areas. Now we don't bother, as if to say, we are not separate from what's here. Drinking iced coffee in Abyss-san's van, we roll past blue hydrangeas, a public bathhouse, a cattle pasture, an apple orchard, and an entire coast of ruins. Humid heat invades the van, dispelling the night's cool mist. There's the old shock of leaving the fully functioning part of town and descending into the dead zone. Flies, gnats, and mosquitoes swarm us. Our windshield smashes a blue butterfly.

Volunteering

Abyss-san watches Nikki reading emails on her smartphone and rolls his eyes. Better to pay attention to whatever is coming before us, he says. A Tweet comes through about people on the Oshika Peninsula who need food, so we decide that it's our turn to be volunteers. We pool our money and find a grocery store. Four thirty-five-pound bags of rice and five bottles of cooking oil, five of soy sauce, handfuls of ginger, onions, carrots, and potatoes are purchased, and we head out for the isolated peninsula, the land closest to the earthquake's epicenter.

From Ishinomaki, we travel east, taking the "Cobalt Highway" even though there are signs that tell us to turn back because of road damage. And soon enough, we do have to turn around and start again, taking the winding, quake-damaged coast road up into the mountains.

A Red Cross tent advertises free clothes; further on, there's a shack with newly washed shirts hung out to dry on a tree. Ayukawa is a controversial whaling town that was totally demolished, except for a sign showing a map of the tip of the peninsula that says "*saru*" (monkeys). Now the monkeys are being collared and used to record radiation levels. A modern hotel high up on a cliff has been shaken into cubist disrepair, its metal fence at the edge all bent, as if every car had gone that way. The road narrows to a tight one-way track, an asphalt ruffle with a broken white line that looks like the sacred Shinto cutouts called *gohei*.

Niyamahama is a village of twenty-five houses built on a hill. A man comes out of his house and waves us down. They're expecting us. Two strapping fishermen help us heft the food boxes up steep steps to the *minshuku*, the town's B&B. The middle-aged owner greets us. She shows us where to stack the donated food. After, we're served green tea and raw octopus at a long table with a young woman who lost her house in another village. Her four-year-old daughter wears a pink dress and, rather compulsively, pulls a matching pink suitcase with wheels back and forth across the floor.

"We didn't want to ask for help, but no one noticed us," the owner says. "People who lost their houses walked here and are staying with me. I've lived here all my life. We've always shared what we have. Now we are sharing the donations—food and money and petrol.

"We are the closest village to the epicenter so we had less time than anyone else between the quake and the tsunami. Luckily, our town is built on a cliff. The Wave didn't come all the way up here. But our harbor was destroyed and everyone lost their boats. Two fishermen got washed off the seawall but they swam back, so no one here died. But down the coast there were stories of fishing boats standing upright in the Wave as they tried to get out, and they drowned.

"After the *jishin,* we got the generator going and I fired up my gas cookers. We boiled water and cooked food until we ran out. The roads were so bad, we couldn't drive to town for three months. One man was so desperate he walked all the way to Ishinomaki to get help."

Nikki, Abyss-san, and I follow the steep road to the tiny harbor. "The only boats you'll see belong to visitors," we're told by a man wiping his neck with a towel. It's hot and muggy. Kelp flies crawl all over our arms, legs, and faces in black masses. An old man and a seagull walk the breakwater. The inlet is narrow and small in circumference, and when the Wave came, it slammed all the boats against the cliff wall, then took the broken bits out to sea. The entire Oshika Peninsula shifted seventeen feet to the east and sank four feet. Seawater splashes over what remains of the wall.

A balding, middle-aged fisherman wearing a white tank top drives his black scooter up and stops near us. "There were forty or fifty boats here and they're all gone now," he says. "My scallop business is finished. I used to get eight hundred thousand scallops per season. I just put sixty tons of scallop seeds out in November. It takes about nine months for them to grow to full size. There're all gone now. It might take ten years to get back to where we were. I spent 80 million yen on boats and equipment. If I could get just 13 million yen from the government, I could get back in business, but that will take a year. The national government has agreed to give us a third of our costs and the rest we pay with low-interest loans. It will take a while. If it doesn't work, this town won't exist anymore."

He looks out at the ocean. "The worst thing is how the ground has sunk and the seawall lifted. We used to be able to drive along the seawall; now we can't do it. Something like this happens once in a millennium. But the worst thing is the nuclear power plant. We have one too, just around the corner here. If the waves had been twenty centimeters higher, the same problem would have happened at the Onagawa plant.

"Our fate all depends on the shape of the coves. Some areas went so fast. Of the four houses on the road to Onagawa from here, only two are left. Right after the earthquake, trees fell across our road and it took a month or so to clear them. Electricity and water took two months. No one works now. The sea floor is covered with debris. Sea urchins are fattening on the dead bodies at the bottom. If you go trolling for flatfish, you might pull out a dead friend."

A man in an out-of-town car drives down to the inlet and heaves a plastic bag of garbage into the sea, then drives away. A hawk dives, pecks open the bag, and eats the flotsam, followed by a huge flock of seagulls.

We walk back to the *minshuku* to say good-bye. The little girl greets us, still pulling her pink suitcase as if ready to evacuate. That's one of the new words she's just learned, along with three others. Her mother asks her to recite them. The girl lifts her face, smiles, and enunciates slowly (in Japanese): "Tsunami, refugee, rebuilding."

Evening Ash

We twist down out of Oshika Honto's high mountains at sunset past villages that have been destroyed, though their hillside graveyards are still standing. "Only the dead survived," I say. A Japanese bush warbler flies in front of the van so close to the windshield, we almost hit it. There are shrines all over Japan where you can ask forgiveness for the inadvertent deaths you have caused: stepping on a bug or hitting a bird with a car. Who will do penance for the subduction zone, for the earth's crust, for the Wave?

More warblers zoom by. On the other side of the road, a woman plucks rice seedlings out of a basket on her back and punches them into a flooded field. As we come into the ruined town of Ishinomaki, there's an acrid smell. "Put the windows up quickly," Abyss-san says. We are passing a crematorium, and the ash of burning bodies is sifting in.

On the way north we stop to see Satoshi-san, the geisha's architect-nephew. Fiftyish, strong-jawed, and handsome, he lives with his Aunt Ito-san, because he is unmarried. He was at work when the earthquake hit. "We were making a final check on an apartment building that had just been completed. I saw a debris pile coming in our direction and smoke, and wooden houses being crushed, so I told the workers to go to a safe area. The toll road nearby was stopped with traffic, and I had to go around the long way.

"By the time I got to an evacuation center, the water hadn't receded, so I stayed there. I didn't know if Ito-san had survived or what had happened to our town. There were no blankets. One propane stove was on and we all put our feet toward it. They gave us newspapers to put over our shoulders. In the night more people came. They were from the town of Kirikiri. Everyone began exchanging stories. We heard that downtown Kamaishi was gone and the whole town of Otsuchi was on fire."

The next morning it took Satoshi-san more than an hour to walk to his aunt's house. When he saw that it had been destroyed, he walked to a nearby school to get something to eat. "That's when I found her, and I've been here ever since," he said.

After applying to the lottery for a temporary housing unit, Satoshi-san recently found out that he and Ito-san can soon move in. "There are two bedrooms, a kitchen, and a bathroom," he says. "We may be in temporary housing for two or three years."

The week before the tsunami he had handed in his resignation at his construction company. They'd asked him to stay on for another month, which he did; then the whole office washed away in the tsunami. He says he isn't going back. "I'm thinking of setting up a small office of my own somewhere. I'd like to help people who want to rebuild. Every person is different, with different-shaped bodies, and every house should be shaped differently. But in the meantime, the government will have to build more houses. This takes time and the longer it takes, the more people will leave and move far away, and our town will die.

"We'll make do for now. There have been many sorrows. We had a mutual friend who was lost in the waves. My aunt was heartbroken. Three days before the *jishin,* she came to visit and brought sweet sake. They didn't know it then, but they were having a drink together for the last time."

In the morning I'm "handed back" to Masumi and her family in Sendai.

* * *

The flow of the river is ceaseless and its water is never the same. The bubbles that float in the pools, now vanishing, now forming are not of long duration: so in the world are man and his dwellings.

—KAMO NO CHOMEI

* * *

The dead know the moment of construction as, also, a moment of collapse. Having lived, the dead can never be inert.

—JOHN BERGER

Islands in the Streams of Story

The sea becomes light, a window is open.

——OZAKI HOSAI

In the seventeenth century a twelve-panel folding screen called "The Waves at Matsushima," painted in ink, powdered color, gold, and silver on thick paper by Tawaraya Sotatsu, shows rows of combers rolling toward shore in seeming unison, parting for each pine-studded island. Under the panel, I read this poem:

Islands and islands
Shattered into a thousand pieces
Summer's sea

Masumi and I are on the morning ferry from Shiogama to Katsura Island plowing through floating debris and blue sparkle. Ahead are islands and islets of red pine and rock, with tiny coves and narrow beaches, as if they had been torn from the mainland, and are now the last remnants of earlier tsunamis.

Looking back, I can see the towns of Shichigahama, Shiogama, Higashi-Matsushima, Nobiru, and Ishinomaki that once lit this sensuous arc of land and are now, for the most part, razed.

We slide by half-ruined shipbuilding factories. A Japanese Navy ship that was used in rescue operations after the tsunami is tied up at a pier. A man explains that the outer islands helped block the inner ones from the Wave. The tiny islets we pass in the middle of the channel are green dots with huge scars where half their mass was removed by roaring water.

Gulls follow the boat and snatch shrimp snacks from children's hands. Fishermen are cleaning debris from the ocean's surface and hauling it in small barges behind their trawlers. One island was home to the lighthouse that showed sailors the way into port. The Wave washed over it and its light no longer shines.

When Matsuo Bashō came to explore Matsushima, he was astonished by its beauty. In *Oku No Hosomichi,* he wrote: "I would like to say that here is the most beautiful spot in the whole country of Japan . . . Tall islands point to the sky and level ones prostrate themselves before surges of water. Islands are piled above islands, and islands are joined to islands . . . "

I snap a picture from the ferry railing. The wind picks up and current lines divide the sea surface into pale blue and ink blue crenulations. Towns recede—they are dark—and the islands ahead are wave-drenched. The farther out we go the more wind-bent the trees. The ferry slows to avoid floating debris; a fishing boat rescues an upside-down skiff with a hole in its hull.

Bashō had a keen eye for unexpected beauty at the moment of destruction. If he'd been here he would have seen islands breaking, fires lighting harbors, snow flying past red pines, humans and houses vanishing in a wave-riddled sea. We turn north and the channel narrows. Ahead, in bright sun, the flower-lined paths of Katsura Island come into view.

The island is shaped like the leg of a chicken, narrowing from thigh to toe. Near the dock fishermen mend oyster beds with long bamboo poles. We disembark. A hand-painted sign shows Bashō's trail. Near the top of a steep hill ravens call out and mosquitoes swarm and bite. We enter a hilltop *jinja* built in 1627 surrounded by a dark cedar forest, and continue on, following the path down the other side. We end up marching right into the middle of someone's garden.

"*Sumimasen,* we are lost," we say to a spry older woman picking vegetables. She waves her hand and says we are welcome to come through. "The tsunami stopped just below our house," she says, resting her hands on the handle of her hoe.

"*Tsunami-wa.* It was taller than that big pine tree," she says, pointing. "The tree next to it was swept toward our house . . . It was snowing that day, and it was hard to see, but I heard a deep rushing noise. The ocean was dirty and kept getting higher."

She accompanies us down the narrow lane. "The water came to here," she says, pointing to a terraced garden just below her house. There's a line of rosebushes in bloom. I ask how this is possible. She says, "The water came in over the beach, and over these flowers, and went out very fast. Not enough time to kill them."

Below this point every house is in ruins. A man walks across the inundated rice field from another hilltop shrine, wiping his eyes. The woman looks at him. "A few people died here, but most survived. We are isolated so we always have food, and there's a spring with a tap, so after the tsunami we could get water." But the seaweed factory over the hill where she'd worked all her life is in ruins. "I'd just retired. I'm seventy, so now we just grow our food and live."

A bird cries. She looks up: "That's a *kiji*, a pheasant. They let us know when an earthquake is coming. They crouch down and press their chests and stomachs to the ground; they can feel it coming. If we see them do this, we know."

At the island school, now an evacuation center for those who lost their houses, we're met by a young Japanese man wearing a Yankees jersey, number 55, Hideki Matsui's number. He comes forward with his hand extended and says hi in Brooklyn-accented English. "I'm Japanese but I went to boarding school in Connecticut, and lived in New York. I produce hip-hop."

He has gathered a motley crew of Japanese musicians from

all over Japan to volunteer in Tohoku. A hefty guy with a long ponytail sits splay-legged under an umbrella and smokes one cigarette after another. He says he's a singer from Kyoto. Two others, barefoot and wearing bright headbands, practice aikido on the lawn.

"We're just musicians who decided to help. This is our statement to the world," the producer says. "Natural disasters can't be stopped, but radiation can. We can say NO to nuclear power. I hope people in this civilization will think harder about where they're going. We are dying from this. We're gathering data about the children of Fukushima, creating a data bank for the future."

A musician from Fukushima City who volunteered to be the cook throws a bowl of yakisoba on the outdoor grill, adds shoyu and cabbage, and bends an ear to listen to it sizzle.

"I believe in the power of music," the young producer says. "We all share the world through it, we all have music inside us. Humans can be a loving animal. This is what the whole world should do—get together and help each other in times like this. We need to face the way of our living, how it has separated us, how it has destroyed the world.

"We've gotten money mostly from America," the producer says. "The Americans always help. Not the Japanese. We organized medical supplies from Direct Relief in Santa Barbara, California, and money from SoftBank in Taiwan." When his cell phone rings, he excuses himself with the aplomb of a strangely dressed CEO.

The singer whispers: "His label is called 'Future Shock.' Pretty cool, huh? Perfect name for all this!" he says, gesturing to the razed coast behind the hill.

Utsumi Kumezo hangs his head out the window of the school and asks if we want a beer. A handsome man in his seventies, he's serious and playful at once. The sun is very hot, almost

100 degrees Fahrenheit, so we gladly go inside. He's chatty and gregarious, at home in his island world, a widower who lost his wife thirty years ago.

"On March 11 I felt something different. I've never felt an earthquake that strong. I knew immediately that the tsunami was coming. So I got the island's fire truck and drove it around to warn everyone. The fishermen went behind me in small trucks, picking people up to take them up the hill. We evacuated everyone to the top of the island. We spent one night up there. The snow made it hard to see the wave. But the next day—it was beyond our understanding. The wave came from the same direction three times. Each time it was higher. It was more than fifteen meters high."

I ask him why he thinks this happened. He tells me that the *kamisama* didn't do this. "It's just the natural way of things. So we can't get angry at anyone. It's just *shizen*—nature. We can't go against nature because we won't win. We must accept what is and just follow it. Nature flows wherever it wants to go.

"I don't have much time left, so I want to do something right now for this island. I thought we needed to do something good, so we're planting cherry trees at people's houses and sunflowers along the lanes. This island is a beautiful place. We all know each other. The flowers are the first step in rebuilding our lives. The flowers are important: a small gesture, but a symbol of being alive."

Mori

Sodden skies and a slight chop on the water of Matsushima Bay. Today the ferry is taking Masumi and me to a small outer island. One islet is a house-sized boulder with a red pine growing out of a crack. We pass small fishing boats heaped with debris rather than fish. Because most ice factories are still inoperable, the government is paying fishermen to clean up the seas.

After several stops we arrive. Except for three women mending fishing nets, the island is deserted. I ask a man with a small boat if he'll take us around. His name is Mori. A brightly polished brass key hung around his neck falls forward as he leans down to start the engine. I ask what it's for, and he says, "My new temporary house."

Mori is shy, sixtyish. An orphan, he was adopted by an islander here. "It's funny. Now I have a home and I'm ferrying orphans and refugees. That makes us all the same," he says with a faint smile.

When the earthquake hit his boat swung back and forth, from side to side in the water. "I couldn't drive it at all!" he tells us. "Finally I came back here, tied up, and ran up the hill just as the tsunami came."

Mori was lucky. Tucked in behind a hill, his twenty-five-foot fishing boat was protected from the Wave. "All the boats parked on the far side of the island were safe. The island cut the tsunami wave in half. Most of it went to the other side of the anchorage."

He looks toward the open ocean: "I heard the noise. Like something breaking. A horrible sound. I saw boards, whole houses, and boats being smashed and washed around. I can still hear it, and see the snow and the broken houses washed together with the ones coming in from other islands. It was awful . . . " But he smiles.

He starts the engine and we putt-putt across a narrow strait to a tiny island: "I'll wait for you," he promises. Houses are built closely together here and, because the ground has subsided, water splashes in and around their foundations. The village seems deserted, then we hear a sound—a woman's voice—and we walk toward her. The first floor of every house holds a few inches of water. We come to a door that opens onto a flooded living room. The furniture is in disarray, and beyond, another door opens to the bay.

We hear the voice again and go through. A lone woman is talking to herself. She squats on wet cement cleaning oyster shells. Small waves splash water over the wall. This whole island is wet.

Wearing traditional work clothes, she looks up, surprised to see us, but her hands never stop: "I'm supposed to be putting the seed of the oyster into the shell," she explains. "But now we missed the crop, so I'm seeing which of these old shells can be reused and which cannot. I clean each one and string them together."

She works alone. Her house is still habitable, she tells us. There is electricity and water, but at high tide, the first floor fills with water. A minor inconvenience, she says. "Every day the tide comes up five feet. I work until it comes in, then I must stop. But the second floor of the house is okay. I want to stay living here, but in the fall the tides will be higher, and this house and all of them along here are sinking.

"We were fifteen families here. Now there are only nine of us. I wasn't on the island when the *jishin* hit, and couldn't get here. There was no ferry for twenty days." She stops to light a cigarette. Her face is wind-chapped. After a few puffs, she flicks the cigarette into the water. Finally she smiles, squats down, takes up a gray shell, scours the inside, and lays it in a heap with thousands of others.

Mori is waiting for us when we return, his bald dome shining in the sun. "Thirty-three years ago there was a tsunami but it didn't damage the houses. This used to be an island where lots of visitors came, and we always had fun. Island people do, you know. But now . . . there's no one . . . It's too quiet," he says, his cheeks going bright red.

Back on the island he offers to drive us up to the evacuation center. "We can borrow one of the pickup trucks. They all have keys in them. Pick one!" I point to one of many small white Toyotas. "Okay. Let's see if she starts." It does, and we climb in back. He drives us up the hill. But the shelter is empty. "I guess they've all gone to the *matsuri*—the festival on the small island over there," he says, nodding toward an arm of land across the water. "I'll take you there in my boat."

It's a short ride. The school celebration consists of relay races, the awarding of trophies, and student speeches given over a microphone on a raised podium. In some towns there have been arguments about whether it's appropriate to have festivals so soon after the disaster, but the islanders here seem to have a sunnier attitude. Why not? Mori says, smiling sheepishly.

I sit on a rock wall under a tree by a man who has a dog on a leash. From there I have a view of the judges' stand where Utsumi, our friend from Katsura Island, looks suave in a pink oxford shirt and a blue blazer. A young girl about to receive an award breaks down and begins sobbing. It's hard to tell if she's faint from the heat or overwhelmed with grief. I ask, but no one around me seems to know.

At the end of the day the school song is sung; then everyone stands and sings the Japanese anthem. After, they raise their fists and shout an enthusiastic "Banzai!!"

An Apprentice Shaman

Jin is not a shaman's apprentice, but an apprentice shaman with wildly radiant eyes, a sturdy body, and a Leica slung around his neck. His images are striking; his shaman-work is coming along. He trained in western Honshu, at a shrine between Nara and Wakayama.

His training was in the old Japanese style: a mixture of Buddhism and Shinto in which the ancestors and *kamisama*—the gods—are one. "The gods are everywhere and divinity lives inside everything. Even those who die are gods," Jin tells me. He also studied an ancient shamanic practice performed mostly by women, the Yuta, of Okinawa. They taught him about curing illnesses and predicting the future. They are the ones who gave him the name Jin.

"When he takes photographs, he uses his given name," Masumi says. "The gallery people who show his work don't know about his occult side. There are lots of people like him around here. It's a quiet network. He doesn't tell people what to do. For us, he's a person who takes the ghosts away. And if I have a problem, I ask him how to resolve it."

Earlier Masumi called Jin from the car as we drove back to Sendai. Her voice was hoarse. He told her it's because she's carrying ghosts on her back, and he will come to Sendai to exorcise them. "He can see into us," Masumi says, wide-eyed. "He helps me identify the powers that are influencing me—a ghost or some kind of karma. I am a person who attracts ghosts. Not everyone does. So Jin helps me. He's the person who takes the ghosts away. He invited me to take photographs with him, and I did. Now I'm getting my doctorate in the history of photography."

Jin carries two old Leicas wherever he goes and shows his work in Kyoto galleries. After the tsunami he plied the coast. Now he wants to take us to the area called Nobiru. "It's just as it was the day after the Wave came," he says. "There has been no cleanup. I want you to see it. It's important to understand that kind of loss."

But first, the ghosts. Masumi lies on the floor of her parents' house and he kneels beside her. Eyes shut, face contorted, he is intensely concentrated. Sweat pours off his forehead, his clothes grow wet. Back straight as a ramrod, he lifts one strong arm above her shoulder, takes a deep breath, expels a loud grunt and a yell, and gives her a soft hit between the shoulder blades. Then another indrawn breath, a raised hand, a hit, a breath, a deep, sonorous exhalation, and the ghosts are gone. As well as the hoarseness in her voice. He is paid the equivalent of $100. After, we drink sake and eat dinner.

Nobiru

"What would you do if you went home and everything was gone?" Jin asks as we drive to Nobiru. "The taxi brings you to your address but there is no house. Your dogs are dead, your horses, and your husband. You find their bodies far away. Your car is crushed. Your library destroyed—all the books strewn, and your work, your notes, and papers. Everything in your world has vanished. You have no money, no job, and no hope of finding one. That's how it is for thousands of people here. Please don't forget that feeling."

We stop and walk. Jin leads the way through abandoned houses. Windows and walls are torn out; bedding and furniture, tatami mats, and frying pans spill from one house into the other. A wall-sized mirror stands in the mud, unbroken. A broom, a pink purse, a calculator, a desk out on the road with all its drawers opened and filled with sand. Two palm trees stand by a ruined house, green fronds beating the air. They survived because they coevolved with tsunamis.

A metronome sits on the sidewalk, its ticking flag bent by the beat of the Wave. Broken plates are scattered. A Seiko watch stopped at 3:45, just after the tsunami hit. There's a tin box marked "Disney Resort," one shoe, three more, a life jacket, a small sake bottle, a CD encased in mud.

Swallows dip and fly. They are mud-lovers, mud-builders. They don't know that this mud is radioactive, and reeks of dead fish, humans, and animals.

Two thousand people died here. One house has fallen sideways into the river. The train tracks at Nobiru railway station are twisted. No trains have come north of Sendai since March and will not do so for a long time. We step carefully between ghosts. We're told that someone in the next village dove down into the water and found three houses completely intact on the ocean floor. No one knows why the cleanup crews have neglected this place.

On a hill above a ruined schoolyard, a well-dressed man says hello. When he finds out I'm American, his face brightens: "Please thank the American Navy for me. They came here right after the tsunami and provided food, clothing, and water to us all. We are way out here and no one else was able to get here because the roads were out. They came from the sea. Our whole town went under the wave. It is upside down now."

We stop at the evacuation center to see a friend of Jin's. "I lost my boat," he tells us. "Some of the fishermen from here were able to drive their boats out. The wall of water was coming at them and they had to move fast. They took their boats up the face of the wave. It was steep and they had to use all their power. The ones who went out too late died. One boat climbed the wave and ran out of gas, but the fisherman just ahead threw him a line and the bigger boat pulled him that way. They both made it. Life or death—it all depends on your destiny, on *kami-hitoe*." He looks at my notebook: "The thinness of the paper you are writing on, that's all that separates any of us from death. The wave here was sixty-five feet high."

Driving again, Jin goes fast. His face resembles a storm. Dark clouds pass over, and sun, then a roiling front creases his forehead and triggers his unsettled mind. I ask about the cast on his arm. "The ligaments in my wrist tore from the bone, just like everything here. Nothing is solid."

Inland from the coast we drive through villages of close-knit houses, still standing but ripped open by the wave. "Look," he says. "The buildings were destroyed but the rock gardens remain. Only the human-made things succumbed to the attack.

"Is Japan worth rebuilding?" he asks. "The spokesman for the government said the radiation will not affect us right away. That's because they won't be in government when people start to die."

On the far coast pink and purple hibiscus line the road. At the very tip of Nobiru, we come upon the village of Tsukihama. A group of people are standing in the middle of the road talking excitedly and hardly notice that we've joined them. They crowd around a man holding a map and pointing at numbered rooms in barrack-like structures. These are the temporary houses the government has built to get people out of the evacuation centers. Once a family has made an application, the houses are doled out by lottery. We've arrived at just the right time: the lottery is *now*.

A middle-aged woman screams in delight. "I just found my house!" she cries out, and runs down the walkway holding her lottery ticket, grabbing my arm to make me run with her. She stops at #206B, looks at her ticket, looks at the number, and screeches: "This is it. We've been waiting three and a half months wondering which house we could have!" She peers in the window and beckons to me to do the same.

"Beautiful," I say. But I can't really see in. When she doesn't open the door I look at her questioningly. "We can't go in yet. We don't have keys."

The "houses" are 550-square-foot apartments in newly con-structed barracks, each with a new refrigerator and TV. The apartments are free, but living expenses are not, which might seem easy enough, unless you've lost your means of making a living.

When we rejoin the group, six people start talking at once, all trying to tell us their tsunami stories. Masumi shakes her head, laughing. "I can't keep up with them."

The head of the community, a middle-aged man with a kind face and a slight belly, takes charge and gives us the village details: "No one here died. We're happy because of that. We were always trained to run to high ground after an earthquake. No matter what. It was getting dark when the tsunami came. It was so cold and everyone gathered together to stay warm. The first wave was only seven meters. The second wave was much bigger, maybe twenty meters, but we didn't see it—we were running."

He continues: "At midnight, there was another tsunami because of an aftershock, but we were still on high ground and safe. We had three evacuation points. We went to the lowest one first, then to the highest. Some people from our village had taken their cars, but they had to abandon them and run. We lost all our possessions but we all survived. Life is more important than those things."

A fisherman groans. Maybe not for him. How will he be able to buy a boat again? The narrow cove where the few village houses and a *minshuku,* a B&B, once stood is completely nonexistent, or at least, nonsensical: a thatched roof lies on the ground, smashed open by two fishing boats that now perch on the open ceiling. Where a house once stood, there's only a spiral staircase left—a corkscrew silhouette leading to nothing.

"Water came from the northwest. Used to be a harbor with lots of boats. The harbor disappeared and the boats sank." Pointing at the strewn timbers of boats and houses, he says, "Nothing will fit together again."

At the top of the road we are met by a gregarious man who introduces himself as Suzuki Kazuo. He looks at the wrecked harbor. "I had gasoline intended for my boat's engine, so after the tsunami we used it to make a fire and cook and stay warm. We owned the small inn in the village. People from the city who wanted to fish came and stayed with us year after year. Now our former customers have been supporting us. It's strange because

I never felt as if I'd been helped by anyone in my life. But now, so many have sent food and money. Such goodness is beyond what I imagined could be. My dream is to build a small house and invite all those who have given to us. I'm sixty-four. Please come back sometime and we'll have tea."

On the way home we are silent. An odd-shaped cloud rises in the north. "Look," Jin says. "That's an earthquake cloud. I'm afraid of the next *jishin*. It will be big and might come soon." If so, will anyone survive?

Finally he smiles. "You have to work hard to change your luck." He stops the car at an evacuation center so we can use the portable toilets. The women are all wearing knee-high rain boots. I ask why. "High tide is coming in. It floods the whole area here. You better hurry up, or you won't be able to get out. You'll have to live with us then!" Laughter. Jin looks at me: "You can't just wait for luck to happen."

We ease back into the evening heat of Sendai, weaving through the usual clotted traffic. The visible past has been erased and the invisible future is an unknown. Water has fiddled with time. The Wave washed into outdoor clocks and softened their mechanisms of precision.

* * *

Desire is inconceivable without a wound.

— JOHN BERGER

Night

Some interior scenes from sleep are too dark to bring into the morning; others ooze out. I'd imagined the devastated coast would be black, but in June, it's dusty; I thought radioactive dust would be red, but it's gray; that hell would be falling ash and hot rocks, but it's moist air and crushed houses. I thought whole forests of bodies would roll onto the beach like cut trees, but they hide, submerged inside waves.

When I was young in California, a mudslide swept neighbors from their bedrooms, and horses from their watering holes. It roared down the *barranca* a few feet from our house. I remember mud, boulders, trees, and water coming down the mountain, and my father's urgent calls to get us up on the hill; how we ran fast with that roar in our ears. A friend's red MG was carried five miles down to Miramar Beach and landed on the sand, upright, the windshield wipers still going. Waves were full of rubbish; whole trees rolled back and forth, their roots still connected; I thought they should be carried back to the mountains and replanted. After, all that was left was a Christmas tree in the creek bed with strings of lights dragging, and my dentist and his wife hanging onto a tree.

Here, in Sendai, I sleep naked on a futon with no blankets, no sheets. My homesickness is a turn of mind that journalists rarely mention but is, I suspect, a constant plague. Before dawn, and its seductive sounds of breakfast preparation, I plot my escape: the bus to Sendai station, the Shinkansen to Tokyo station, the train to Narita, and a plane going home.

I write to my lover, a former war correspondent, and ask him if I've been so thoroughly radiated here by nuclear fallout that I've gravely endangered my health and our happiness together. Have I acted rashly for no reason? Is it another kind of betrayal to stay? Is it a betrayal to all those who suffered here to leave?

Twenty-three years ago in northeastern Japan, my friend Leila and I spent weeks talking to *itako*—blind mediums who communicate with the dead. Rubbing a long rosary, an *irataka-juzu* with its three hundred black soapberry beads interspersed with bear claws and teeth, one *itako* went into a trance and told me things she couldn't have known about my dead friend. After, we climbed the northeastern mountain of Osorezan to see where the *itako* go to speak to the dead in the summer. It was midwinter and the snow was knee-high. The Shinto-Buddhist cosmology of the dead is described as a hot hell with dry riverbeds full of dead children, ponds of blood, hills of swords, a beach of paradise, and a red bridge that connects heaven and hell, the living with the dead.

Now ghosts float all over the Sanriku coast and I wonder if a path is being worn straight through to that peak. Sunlight filters through *shoji* and day comes on. Debris piles unravel, but no one can remember how to remake what was here, how a whole society of interlacing families, friends, obligations, and habits is made; what a bicycle looks like, or a bed, or a door.

Lying half on, half off the futon, my heels rub the grain of the tatami. Once it was grass waving in the breeze; now it is cut, tied, squeezed, bound, and dead. I lift up, and as I do so, the cupboard doors begin to shake: for a few minutes a violent tremor holds us. *What kind of embrace is this?* A second later, rain explodes as if passing clouds had been punctured; gray cloud-heads tumble down, concussing the ground. The back of my hand lands on the *o-bento*—a box lunch brought from the train.

A day is a box in which earthquakes occur.

Sorrow

Midday, and a man in his sixties who is crying walks down the hill from a small shrine dabbing his eyes. He crosses over flattened houses, picks his way through debris, skirts the blue bins where harvested seaweed was washed, and steps over a battered surfboard, a halved bicycle. Beyond, the beach and the ocean. A few battered skiffs have washed up on shore. He walks and doesn't see.

He approaches. Even three months after the disaster, people still need someone to listen. He tells me how once the houses stood close together with a narrow, flower-strewn path between, how sounds of the *shakuhachi* haunted moon-viewing nights. Garden plots had onions, cabbage, and daikon that shook green into the air. In winter, farmers sang *jinku*—old-fashioned songs. No one was rich but fish, fresh water, flowers, fruit, and food were abundant. And there was no Wave.

Now the tide keeps washing nothingness onto shore. Nothingness and dead bodies. Not long after the tsunami, the Dalai Lama came to visit Japan. The monks accompanying him recited the Heart Sutra 100,000 times, and he talked about the union of emptiness and bliss. But this old farmer says he keeps seeing things as they *were*, not as they are now, and doesn't know how to stop the ghostly procession. He wonders if he's been dreaming. He looks, but there is no focus. He can't tame his mind to what is before him.

Instead, he sees the thronging population of this town and the very places where rogue waves came bearing ships, mud, and trees. He sees arms flailing and heads going under in swirling seas thick with broken boats and clothes. He hears a baseball game get swallowed up by the earthquake's shuddering. He sees where his own house once stood, and how his children ran home from school, calling for the dog, calling for something to eat. He wonders what his wife would be cooking for dinner now if she were alive.

The old man squats down on wet pavement. Already water is coming up around his rubber boots. He pushes the white mask back up on his head and dips a finger into the tide's foam, as if what he's lost might bump by. He carried the bodies of his family in a wheelbarrow to the back door of the crematorium. It too was partly damaged by the tsunami, so they could cremate only one body at a time. The ashes of this whole town's dead coat the water. His daughter. Her child. His devoted wife. His mother.

EMPTINESS FALLS

Beginning. Again. But how?
Tonight's perfect moon-slice means
we are half here half gone.
Down deep sea urchins fatten on corpses
and the Missing roll in on amnesia's tides.
All summer the body rains sweat and
emptiness falls from the standing dead.
Cedar. Rice field. Pine.

Hirayama's Blog

June 30

Thinking back to March: I took my boat out. When I came back in, my house was gone. There were no people. Was anyone alive? I saw smoke. There were fires—out on the water and in what was once our town. But still, no one. The last big tsunami like this was in the Edo period. I never thought this would happen in my lifetime. Today, three months later, we moved into temporary housing. There is no air. The windows don't open. The instructions say we have to have the air ducts open all the time or we'll die from oxygen starvation. So, we survived the tsunami, but they can't make a house that is safe for us to live in now.

August 3

Came home from fishing and the temp house is hot!! Even with the windows and doors open. If the heat gets any worse living in this prefab is going to be tough. It's very different from a normal house. We have to live the best way we can. There are ants inside, and things don't work. Every temp house has its own set of problems.

August 5

Today Sanriku Bay was foggy and hard to see through. Heavy southern winds were blowing and the sea was rough. With the quick waves the boat catches more underwater debris than before and gets caught on it more often than we did right after the tsunami. Why now, I wonder? It's bizarre. If we get caught now, what's going to happen when they start trawling?

August 6

My son's school has open pool classes during the summer holiday. The gym next to it, called the Sea Arena, is still an evacuation center, but it will close on the 10th. People must move into their temporary housing by then. It's a little sad to be separated from all the victims from our town. Volunteers won't be able to visit people and help out anymore, or send donation goods to evac points either. Now it's the job of the volunteer organizations to pass the goods forward. Thank you so much to everybody who has helped us.

The city is deciding whether or not to clear away the broken houses and refuse left behind. I really encourage people to see the disasters for themselves. It's sad, but please come to see it and remember the sight. You may not be able to accept it, but there is a huge difference between witnessing and not witnessing with your own eyes.

August 10

Out on the waves today. The ice factory at Denzaki Wharf has been completed and is running again. The Bonito and Tuna Fishing Associations have requested the Miyako fish market to receive their catch. There are only limited places where there is ice available, since the ice factories were destroyed too. If boats can load up on ice here, more boats will arrive and it will bring back some liveliness to the place.

Came home after work and IT IS SO HOT. 33 degrees C. outside. Inside the house is like a sauna. We have the windows and doors open but there is no breeze. Oh man . . .

August 11

Five months since that day. It seems that time has stopped inside me since then. Parts of me cannot accept reality, some things I don't want to admit yet, and there are some struggles in my heart.

Looking down at Kuwagasaki Bay from the big bridge above Octopus Bay makes me sad. March 11 was when everything changed. Some people had their lives destroyed; some have no hopes or dreams, only despair; some lost their family, home, and jobs. As days go by, you can tell the difference between those who were victims of the tsunami and those who weren't.

Everybody moved into temporary housing today. The evac center where we all lived as a group is now closed. There are still many problems and issues to deal with, and the reality of the world to face from now on.

I've brought my son to the bridge. It's almost 2:46 p.m. That's when the earthquake happened. The waves came at 3:24. It's been five months. The wounds in my heart have yet to heal. I wonder if there will be a siren. A moment of silence.

August 14

I couldn't hear with my left ear and my head started hurting, my face swelling. Went to the hospital for a CT scan. My brain had a swelling. Went home with some medications.

August 18

Another CT scan and the swelling is gone. It seems that all the fatigue and stress caused my brain to be affected by a virus. Not serious. Relieved.

August 24

Our temporary housing unit received clothing from World Vision Japan. Thank you!

August 26
   Back to work. Will go out to sea tomorrow.

August 29
   Lots of flying fish jumping out of the water. Finished the day's catch and unloaded at the market. Great!
   Worried about typhoons, the low air pressure and the waves. It could easily go over the walls and send the boat crashing into the concrete. Might have to sleep over on the boat. So worried.

Radiation News

Five thousand, two hundred tons of stone from the town of Namie were quarried and used to build condominiums for refugees from the no/go zone. The stone is all radioactive and has to be removed.

The latest analysis shows that xenon-133 began to vent from the nuclear plant just after the earthquake, but before the tsunami, though TEPCO still claims the plant was "earthquake safe."

Back home, an earthquake rattled the coast near my rented island house. The nuclear power plant nearby may have been damaged. A few days later, I hear that my house lies in the direct path of an approaching hurricane. The island is evacuated and for a week, I'm not sure if I've joined the ranks of the homeless. The newspapers say that if the earthquake and hurricane had occurred on the same day, another Fukushima-type disaster might have happened. "You might as well move to Japan!" Masumi tells me.

* * *

Masumi's grandmother: "I don't know where I am. I miss my house. Why am I here? When am I going home?"

September

September 11

To breathe is all that is required.

As if not beautiful enough, the wrinkled ocean smooths its own skin. Wave follows wave. It's been six months since the earthquake, tsunami, and nuclear meltdown, and everywhere in Japan there are ceremonies commemorating the dead.

At 2:46 p.m. a moment of silence is observed. Buddhist monks chant the Heart Sutra and the parents of dead children fly paper cranes. In the town of Higashi-Matsushima thousands of candles are lit. In Ishinomaki and Otsuchi white paper lanterns with flickering candles are sent afloat on rivers. In what was Rikuzentakata, a town that vanished in twelve minutes, a memorial service for the city's dead is held in its one remaining hillside temple. After, a bonfire is lit. The blaze is encircled by cut cedar boughs and bamboo poles hung with *gohei*—sacred white papers cut in zigzag shapes (not unlike images of lightning) that represent the presence of the *kamisama*. Divinity resides everywhere.

The euphoria of survival evident in June is now tinged with despair. A futureless future looms. The exact way to live with grief and resurrect one's life and livelihood is in no way clear. No one who lost a house is being allowed to rebuild in the tsunami zone. Instead, they live in temporary housing and plant winter vegetable crops; a few try to remake their homes out of rubble. The ruined coast spins out black haze. Crematoriums have been rebuilt and the dead are sent to the fires, their ashes set under polished granite gravestones, as if something of them might stay.

Sputtering rain and *shuushi*—a word whose two characters represent "fall" and "thought," meaning the lonely feeling of autumn—that's what it's like today. My September Hana Fuda card features *kiku*—chrysanthemum—a flower used for funerals. Outside the Sendai grocery store where we stop to buy peanuts and beer, a pony stands in a small enclosure munching hay. A lone child steps forward, extends his hand toward the soft muzzle. To touch the living; to ingest the smell of horse and hay.

Oceans are depicted in ancient paintings in mesmerizing continuums of moving water, and it's no wonder why. Major earthquakes and tsunamis have occurred in Tohoku for so long, its ground-shakes and waves are a kind of geo-religious ritual. There was the huge tsunami of 1869, one in 1933 that destroyed Kamaishi Bay, and quakes in 1968, 1978, 2005, and 2008. I'm trying to see the lonely beauty in this wreckage, the frozen moment of its undulating rubble, itself a kind of wave.

The unshackled, the undecorated, the rusting, the collapsed, the disentangled, and the bent—it's all here—an alphabet to make a double soup: one, a dark broth of the dead, and the other, swirled on top, a foamy stream of space and beauty.

Today the ocean sparkles, its waves coming in small lopsided loops, and the Kitakami River, where so many died, is dotted with white egrets hunting for fish in the reeds.

Far from this coast a massive mat of Tohoku debris is crossing the Pacific Ocean, replete with secret tsunami stowaways: Pallas's rosefinch, *Carpodacus rosen*, native to China, Japan, and the Korean peninsula. They are using the flotilla to migrate to other islands. It's thought that the precursors of the Hawaiian I'iwi, the scarlet honeycreeper, arrived on Maui and Nihau this way some 5.7 million years ago, and diverged into more new species once Oahu emerged from the sea.

The debris island was discovered by a Russian sailing ship, the *STS Pallada*, whose captain reported that it took seven days to sail through the streaming wreckage, reckoned to weigh between five and twenty million tons. At this writing, Midway Island and Hawaii are behind it, and Alaska, British Columbia, and Washington are ahead. Of the two hundred thousand buildings that were destroyed in northeastern Japan, some remnants, including furniture, house beams, a television, and oyster buoys, a whole house, several pairs of severed feet still encased in running shoes, and a fishing boat with the name "Fukushima" written on the bow, are drifting, seeking a new home.

Ishinomaki and the River

Masumi and I drive north to Ishinomaki. We're on our way back to Shounji to visit the abbot and Fukan-san. Inland from the coast, rice harvest has begun, late because fields had to be tested for radiation. If left husked, rice stays fresh longer, so villagers buy it that way, and take small bundles as needed to the local farm store to get it hulled for 100 yen, a little more than a dollar.

The road parallels the Naruse River near where Masumi's other uncle lives. "As soon as the earthquake came he and his wife packed the car and drove to the top of the nearest hill," she says. "It was snowing and they couldn't see the wave. He simply told his wife to keep checking the snow as they were driving, that if it turned black, it meant that the water had reached them, that there was water under the wheels. They made it to a high spot and wrapped themselves in blankets in the car. There was a knock on the window. The people who lived at the very top saw them and took my uncle and aunt into their house."

Masumi recalls that when she entered an evacuation center looking for them, it was in chaos: "Women were screaming and crying. They had just found their loved ones, or had just lost them. I asked where we might find my uncle—he works in the medical clinic and people know him. One old woman said, 'Please, you mustn't have hope for him.' As I walked out of the center, I heard a woman crying, 'I tried and tried, but I couldn't hold his hand any longer and he disappeared.' "

Masumi found her uncle's name on the survivors' list but still couldn't locate him. "I went back several times. For one week there was no contact between us. He didn't even know that the family house where he grew up had washed away."

We pass the huge Red Cross Hospital. "The smaller clinics and hospitals close to the coast were destroyed, so everyone was moved here. Very quickly they ran out of clean sheets and medicines. I found my uncle there. His own clinic had been ruined, so right away he came to this hospital to help."

We roll past rice farms, uncut blond stalks bending in the wind, and follow a long river from its mountain fastness to the water-gutted houses that are still standing, and to the ones that are not. Where the corner of a bed juts out an empty window, two crows sit on the sill.

A rumor is floating around Japan that another earthquake will come soon. A journalist in Tokyo told me he'd heard it too, but can't find the source. "It comes from the Internet," Masumi says. "A woman from Iwate Prefecture writes a blog. She's a *kamisama*. You know, an *uranaishi*—a fortune-teller. I check her blog every day. There's a big *jishin* predicted for September 26. As big or bigger than the 9.0." She looks at me with an odd grin: "You'll still be here for it," she says. Laughter.

Typhoon clouds amass in the south like a black hedge, but here, it's achingly hot and humid, as if the blanket of heat was trying to suppress oxygen. Near the coast a sour wind bends tall grass until its feathery tops flatten on the ground. The shore is marked by jackknifed pines.

"Earthquakes happen when Mars is on the move," Masumi says. "Two weeks ago there was a 6.8 at 2:43 p.m.—almost exact same time as the big one." Not far from Shounji Temple, the river appears and turns, and we follow its blue trail. Seagulls bob, two men stand on the high levee fishing. "Fishing!" Masumi screeches. She's incensed. "How could they? The river is full of the dead!"

We look for the young woman the abbot told us about: the one who digs for her lost child with a backhoe and searches tirelessly for the missing children from Ookawa Elementary School. We scan the river but see no one. On the other side of the road farmers stake their flowers and vegetables, bracing for the oncoming storm.

At the fork that leads to the temple, I ask Masumi to stop the car so we can climb the levee. I want to see this river where the dead were pulled by grieving relatives out of the mud. She looks agitated, but says nothing. I climb the steep bank and she follows me. The sun is hot, the river is wide, the water is aquamarine. Great white egrets land in trees and preen; ducks swim in and out of reeds. A lone fisherman walks upstream carrying his pole.

On the far shore, dredges are anchored near a road. Naomi, the backhoe woman, is nowhere to be seen. It's an earthen levee, flat on top. Instead of the ash of a charnel ground that I'd expected to find, there's only green grass waving.

The past situation has just occurred and the future situation has not manifested itself. In the gap between the two, the river flows. It passes through, continuously moving. The river is both time and space. I look upstream and down. Today there's a slight chop on the water. The river is where breathing and dying do their jig.

Something startles me: Masumi is running down the steep bank to her car, swatting at her left shoulder. She opens the door and reaches in for something. I see salt flying, salt being broadcast from an upturned palm, flicked by the thumb into the air. With it she quickly anoints her head, shoulders, and back, dabbing an extra pinch onto her tongue. She gasps audibly. I run to her: "I felt something on my back," she yowls. "I have a ghost. There's a ghost on me now!"

I try to calm her but she becomes more fitful, holding her head and yelling: "I don't want to be in these places. I don't want to do this work for you!" We are early for our visit with Fukan-san, so I suggest we roll up our windows, turn the AC on, and drive inland from the river.

Clouds swirl as the predicted typhoon begins its long journey from the Pacific Ocean northward. Here, it's quiet. We follow a narrow valley to a pond called Fujinuma with a tucked-away village on the far eastern shore. Rice fields are still inundated from the tsunami waters, and farmhouses are swamped. We see where the Wave erased boundaries, where ponds turned into bodies of water that moved, and roads disappeared. Houses filled and floated like boats; boats were tossed into forests and hung from trees, and freshwater fish were taken out to sea.

I tell Masumi I want to see Kannonji, the temple behind Ookawa Elementary School that was washed away. She says she can't do it and I ask her to be brave and please drive. She goes fast on the dirt expanse, not looking. We race past the open-air shrine to the lost children, past the school's twisted ramp that leads to hollowed-out interiors, and beyond to where the forest comes down to ribbed bulldozer tracks that lead to the temple's foundation: all that remains of Kannonji. Stay here, I'll be back, I say to her. She locks the doors after I get out. For a moment I wonder if she'll be there when I return.

I walk through the temple's nonexistence, its incensed air, its secret font, its shadowed recess, to the ancient cemetery with its seven or eight headstones—those of earlier temple priests—high enough on the hill so no floodwaters have ever reached them. I walk through nothingness; no boundaries exist. I give the ghosts a pair of legs to walk on.

When I return Masumi is there, but her voice is high and hoarse. I get in the passenger seat. "If I have a ghost with me, my left eye gets smaller and the scar on the top of my eyebrow gets bigger . . . Can you see it?" she asks and turns to me. "Look at my eyes. Can you see that my face is different?" I tell her

I can't really see anything. Do ghosts need to be scary? I ask. Shouldn't we, instead, try to make them feel at home? I tell her about the ghost at the Wyoming ranch where I once lived, the sound of clomping up and down stairs at night, the shot glass of whiskey I left at the landing, and fruit and flowers. Nothing works. It's time to go to Shounji.

* * *

Fukan-san makes tea in the corner of the temple. We sit on tatami. She says that when she arrived in early April, "there were coffins everywhere. So many of them, I couldn't count, but maybe a hundred dead people outside, around the big tree. Some coffins didn't have lids. It looked like a courtyard full of zombies . . . I'm sorry, I shouldn't say things like that . . . but I was so scared. The bodies had been taken from the river and their wet clothes were in plastic bags. When I saw all this I began shaking. The situation was too awful. Some people saw neighbors' kids hanging in trees. Other children were discovered buried in the mud, just a hand showing. People saw many things and it's hard to erase those terrible sights from the mind.

"My uncle, the abbot, looked exhausted. He was writing the names of the dead on the sacred sticks. His room was full of them. There had been people living here at the temple in the early weeks after the tsunami, but they were gone. From then on, it was just funeral after funeral.

"After I put my things away, I thought I better go out and see what had happened to the villages. I went by bicycle. The houses I had known when I visited as a child were either washed away or broken. I saw upside-down cars in a rice field and huge trees knocked down, and a greenhouse broken to bits. People were getting whatever they could of their personal belongings, and volunteers were shoveling mud. I had only sandals on and it was hard to make my way. The asphalt was broken apart and deep mud covered everything. Finally my bicycle came to a halt. I rode back here and soon, I was conducting funerals."

Young and robust, Fukan-san is slated to take over the duties of the abbot, who is in bad health, when he can no longer serve the *sangha*. She leans in close and whispers: "My mother wanted me to be a hairdresser. I have a beautician's license!" she says, grinning. "I know how to cut hair." I look at her shaved head and break out laughing. "That life wasn't for me, so I became a nun." More laughter. Was that your only other choice? I ask. Laughter again.

There's a long silence. Candlelight flickers across the photographed faces of tsunami victims. I ask how many funerals she has conducted. She says she can't remember, there have been so many. "Hundreds died in the farming communities around here, and now we've merged with the Kannonji community, and we have the ashes of a hundred more."

All afternoon mourners file past. Two young mothers bring photographs of their dead children to place on the altar. They are very matter-of-fact about it: "We finally got them framed," they say, smiling. We look at the faces of the children and nod. The women put the photographs on the altar under the urns of ash. We light sticks of incense. They bow to Fukan-san and leave.

A family group comes in talking and laughing. Paying one's respect to the departed is now routine. Another family, more solemn, approaches Fukan-san—the father, mother, and two children—and they prostrate before her. She remains expressionless, waits for them to rise, and returns the bow.

Others come and go while we sip tea. A few are crying. They hold hands tightly and smile. A lone woman lays a bouquet of sunflowers wrapped in newspaper near the front doors, with the blossoms facing us.

I'd thought earlier that I would want to talk to these people, but what would the conversation be? The steady procession says it all. They are grieving; Fukan-san shares in their pain.

Fukan-san continues: "There's a gap between the people who lost family and those who didn't. The police kept saying don't touch the dead, but the families knew to just act directly. The woman with the backhoe is still digging for her daughter. You can go look for her near Ookawa School, or on the river. She might be there today.

"In the early days after the tsunami, the families pulled their dead out of the river, and brought them all the way up here from the mud. It's hard to know how to behave until you are in that situation. Those are moments of true feeling, of true behaving, and we must not forget them.

"Some days I thought I didn't understand Buddhism well enough," she says. "But I learned two things: we have to behave as humans and feel the situations as they come before us. Every day is important. No regrets. This is all we have."

Autumn Equinox

Masumi sleeps with two cups of salt at the head of her bed and a long hunting knife above the pillow. We're at her parents' house in Sendai again. There's one ghost on her, she says, and there may be one on me; she's trying to protect herself from acquiring others. She calls Jin, the shaman, who lives in Shizuoka, seven hours' drive south of Sendai, but he says he can't come. A cool mist stirs into the day's heat and humidity, and flies, gnats, and mosquitoes roar around. Like all of us, they float through wind-driven layers of dust and radioactive particles.

It's the autumnal equinox, when people in Japan clean the graves of their ancestors and place cut flowers on them. According to Shinto beliefs, the dead need affection. Even after death they continue to be a "living" presence in the household. They are demigods, guarding the house and instructing young and old in matters of moral rectitude. But the untethered dead, the unclaimed, are fearsome ghosts, longing to reattach themselves to the living, polluting the sanctity of blood ties, of loyalty to household, community, and livelihood.

The loyal bonds to family, called *kizuna,* must be guarded, not severed. The family itself becomes a religion conjoined with a deep sense of belonging to place. Some days, it must be a balm for those times when we feel lost and alone; other times, I wonder if it doesn't seem like a prison.

Another earthquake comes as the Pacific plate bulges and rolls back down into Earth's mantle. Earth's grand way of recycling.

Each terrestrial movement reflects a shift in the mind. A jolt and a lurch and I grab the edge of the futon. The mirror shakes so hard I can see only a shattered, cut-up version of my eyes looking for a body, a room.

The ocean is a bright edge that keeps trying to bring time and life back around, but its credibility has been marred. Who can trust it to move anyone here into the future? There are 5.7 and larger earthquakes every day, and there's a typhoon on the way. September's seismic brain is a cranial nook jolted and cushioned by bone.

Because it is still hot and humid, face masks have been discarded and we get respiratory infections. Japan's air has been corrupted. We breathe it in. We eat produce grown in sandy, radiation-swallowing dirt. We carry the dead and the broken inside our bodies; we carry ghosts and hydrogen explosions; we take them with us; we take them home.

Early morning. A slight shake. The grinding-firing of Earth's mantle polishes itself into a mirror. Autumn is on the way. Nothing will shine then. All will drive toward the subdued, reduced to the rust of the season, its beautiful desolation.

A farmer tells me that at this time of year the nuts of ginkgo trees ripen and heavy persimmons fall from trees. Two hundred thousand sunflowers, thought to absorb radiation, are still blooming in Hokkaido. TEPCO is trying to stem the flow of radiation from its stricken plants but so far has failed. Cell phones will soon be equipped with dosimeters—radiation detectors. Scientists ponder the effect of global warming on seismology. The earth's crust may be more fragile than it first appeared, so when glaciers shrink or break off, the realignment of Earth may result in violent tremors.

Great-Uncle and Great-Aunt

Kazuko, Masumi's mother, stands in the ruins of Grandmother's house—her childhood home, once a big, two-story farmhouse that looked out on the family's rice fields. She is cutting the red Gerber daisies her brother planted. When the last flower is snipped, she stands straight, holding the bundle, when something catches her eye. She spins on her heels: "They're here! Look!" She drops the flowers to the ground and runs over the bridge to the half-ruined house of her uncle and aunt. Tears stream. She has not seen them since the disaster.

We stand at the long veranda of the traditional Japanese house. The interior is in ruins: there is no glass in the windows, only parts of a subfloor, and no sliding doors. From the shadows Great-Uncle Satoru comes forward, wiping dirt from his face. He is bent all the way over in an L from osteoporosis and has trouble walking. His wife, Satsuko, appears. She's ten years younger, with a farmer's robust body, rough hands, and a beautiful face.

Kazuko, Masumi, and I bow. Emotions spin: everyone is sad, happy, uneasy. We step up into the open room. No need to take off our shoes. When the tsunami roared through, it tore away all the tatami. The *moya*—the miniature Shinto shrine meant to protect the dwelling—has been dug out of the mud and returned to an alcove. A Danish modern table and four chairs brought by volunteers sits in one corner so covered in dust we could write our names on it.

"We're very tired," Satsuko says. "We've just finished planting our crop of winter vegetables. We ride our bicycles here from our temporary apartment because the tsunami took our car. That's why we haven't been able to visit you on the other side of Sendai."

On the table there's a thermos of tea and two sets of discarded work gloves. A *jyoren*—a heavy, old-fashioned hoe—lies on the floor. We sit in stunned silence. The house seems unreal, as if we were on a stage set. This exhausted couple are the players.

Great-Uncle Satoru sits bent with his head tipped down. He rubs his forehead, obviously agitated. A wind picks up. Through its wounds and openings, the house receives all the dirt and rain that the ruined coast can give.

Eleventh-century *emaki*—scrolls that illustrated the *Tale of Genji*—were rendered with a *fukinuki yatai*, "roof blown off" perspective. Every room was open to the omniscient viewer from the top down so that the intimate happenings of palace lives and the characters' interconnections were revealed. Here, the roof is on, but with no windows or doors, the interior can be seen from the side, at ground level. Either way, there is no privacy.

Before the tsunami the houses of this extended family were linked: Kazuyoshi and his wife lived with his parents in front; Great-Uncle Satoru and his family lived in back, on the other side of the channelized river. Now the view from Satoru's house is all crumbled foundations and nothingness—a scene of utter destruction. The ocean glints beyond.

In the distance a fire breaks out: it is the mountain-sized debris pile catching fire. Heat has caused internal combustion. It is over 100 degrees Fahrenheit with 100 percent humidity. Three orange cranes use their buckets to squash the arrowing flames.

Yesterday, working alone, Satsuko and Satoru covered the salty tsunami-rinsed soil with seventy bags of manure and planted seedlings ordered from a nursery in Yokohama: green onions, bok choy, peas, and broccoli. Then they watered each plant by hand.

"Uncle won't eat anything bought at the store," Great-Aunt says. "He's losing weight. We have to plant these vegetables quickly."

She shows us where water rose inside the house to within five inches of the ceiling, and the upper corner of the room where the Wave drove through like a sharpened spear. "We were watching the tsunami from the *nikai* [the second floor]," Uncle Satoru says. "I heard the voice of the water. Of the ocean and that small river. It told me to run but it was too late. We were so scared. Our son was with us. He was angry because we hadn't left for the evacuation center. He had been watching the river and saw that the water didn't look right. It seemed weird, he said. The water got high very quickly. He yelled at us to run upstairs. We did. But even so, the water lapped at our heels.

"Right then, we thought we would die. The first wave wasn't too big, and when it pulled back so fast, we were sure the next one would take us. It didn't, but it took my sister's house just in front." He points toward the foundation where his sister's house should be. "We watched it disappear. It happened so fast. The roof came off and it was floating. Our house and the ones behind us are the only ones that didn't wash away.

"Night came. Some of our neighbors were sitting on their roofs. The Japanese army came in helicopters, but all the lights of Sendai were out and it was hard for them to see us. We tried to get on the roof too, but we couldn't because of our age. So our son went up and waved his flashlight. They found us that way.

"We heard the helicopter over us. A soldier came down to the roof on a rope and climbed into the second floor. He put a harness on each of us and, one by one, pulled us up into the helicopter. We were lucky that way. The people in the evacuation centers were cold and had no food, but we were taken to the army base and fed and kept warm.

"We stayed one night. After, we went to the evacuation center, where we lived for a month. In the beginning there was not enough food, but the PTA and the principal of the school asked farmers from inland areas to provide rice and vegetables. A month later, we moved to the little apartment where we are still."

Great-Uncle Satoru rests his head on his hand, his posture one of defeat. His voice is tired and sad. "I grew up here. I spent my entire life here. We always grew our own rice and vegetables and flowers. We had lots of room, lots of space. The apartment where we live now is very small. I feel crazy there. So I ride my bicycle over here and meditate!"

We go outside to look at the garden. The rows are about forty feet long, roughly hewn, with tiny seedlings tucked into white salt-encrusted dirt. Two flats of flowers are yet to be planted. "I *need* the food," Great-Uncle Satoru says, "but I *have* to have flowers."

The wind kicks up with more determination: smoke and dust from the burning debris vent directly into our faces. There's no way to avoid it. We sit placidly. Great-Uncle Satoru lifts his head and becomes more animated: "Because this house is still standing, I want to live here again, but the city of Sendai has not given us permission yet. I have a right to rebuild and live here. I'm seventy-five years old. I don't care if another tsunami comes and takes me. The government gives money to the people who lost their houses, but not if the house is still standing. The rebuilding will be very expensive. If the government decides you can't rebuild on the land, they won't give you any money at all. It's a great inequity.

"This house protected our lives. But the government is in a gray zone. They didn't take this area into consideration. The other side of the river, where my sister's house once stood . . . they are sure no one can rebuild there. Too dangerous. But here, where there are still houses standing . . . there are many who want to stay but we have no leader.

"We Japanese tend to be too polite, so the government doesn't do anything." He looks at me, smiling faintly. "You Americans who immigrated from so many parts of the world are better at this than we are. We have to change how the country is ruled. And right now, I want the answer. Yes or no. But I won't live anywhere else."

Sendai

Inland from the coastal zone farmers are harvesting rice, their golden sheaves laid along bamboo poles and left to dry. Men and women are planting winter vegetables in every spare piece of land. How else will they eat? A few miles from the coast, house repairs are going on, and people are buying used cars from small lots along the road.

As we go through the city, Masumi says she'll never park her car on the rooftop lot at the Sendai station again, because those cars shook against each other so violently, not a piece of metal was left undented. Closer to the coast the Wave took the rest, one by one, street by street, bridge by bridge, and cars were hurled and tumbled, sometimes sinking with the drivers still in them. In Kesennuma alone, two hundred people were killed in a single parking lot. Now, homeless and jobless, the survivors walk or ride bikes to their farm fields. One hundred years of modernization seem to have been erased in one afternoon.

Central Sendai is a different story. It's a stately city with tree-lined avenues, tall hotels, and Parisian-style stores that bespeak affluent Japan's worldly tastes.

Kazuko and I wander through an elegant department store. Earthquake damage to buildings here has long since been repaired. Looking for a way to spend an hour, we thumb through fall fashions, Ralph Lauren jodhpurs, tall boots, heavy sweaters, ceramic teapots, makeup, and earrings. On the bottom floor, Kazuko buys imported meat, cookies, and coffee, and after, we pass through Tiffany's to browse "eternity" rings on the way out of the store. Diamonds and rubies, or sapphires? Which do I prefer? she asks. From the ruins of her childhood neighborhood to this store: it's a jolt and a wonder, and we laugh about it. I suggest they change the name of the rings from "eternity" to *mokka*, at this moment. Now.

We walk the avenue under grand old trees in evening heat. Impermanence is a living experience, a rolling of the dice, a chance-dance, a breaking down of what seemed solid: kitchen, boat, car; wedding ring, child, lover; the annual cleaning of graves. True existence is nothing but nosedives and quick gulps of air, as Earth flexes her geologic muscles. In one minute, everything can change. Seashore to charnel ground; charnel ground to dance ground where the play of living and dying keeps taking place.

On the evening news we're told that the three damaged reactors at Fukushima Daiichi are almost ready for "cold shutdown," though that hasn't happened yet, and radioactive water still streams into the Pacific. Hotspots are being found far south and west of the site. Airborne particles hit high buildings and mountains and fall in place. Wind, waves, and currents carry the radiated water up and down the coast, first north, then south, changing seasonally.

Kayuko, Grandmother, and Kazuyoshi

Early evening, almost dark, and raining again. "The windshield has tears," Masumi says, laughing. We're going to visit Masumi's aunt and uncle. Dropping down from the highway to her aunt's rented garden plot on the river, we take photographs of the tall sunflowers that separate her vegetables from other plots. "Growing food is what she knows how to do," Masumi says.

The last time we visited their temporary house, only Masumi's uncle, Kazuyoshi, was there. Now, only her aunt Kayuko is home. She greets us with a smile. Lines radiate from her eyes like sprays of light. Her hair is cut short and hennaed reddish-brown; her freckled tan looks permanent. She has only one upper tooth. It twists and pushes forward, pointed like a short spear. She apologizes that Kazuyoshi isn't around. Perhaps we don't want to bother talking just to her, but I protest: "No, no, we've come to talk to *you*!"

The apartment is spacious but almost bare. Just a low table and a few cushions. Grandmother is tucked in an alcove in a hospital bed. "She arrived today," Kayuko explains. Masumi's mother and I pay our respects and sit down.

Kayuko fumbles with tea and hot water, eventually serving us only *sayo*—hot water—because, somehow, she is unable to get the tea made. Grandmother appears to be sleeping, but she's not. As soon as she hears a cookie being unwrapped, she bends her hand into the shape of a horn and bellows out: "I'm hungry!"

Kayuko smiles, and informs us that she has a feeding tube and should be full.

We sip hot water from tea bowls. Kazuko gives Kayuko an apron from Fujisaki—one of Sendai's fancy department stores. She shakes it out and holds it up high, smiling and thanking her sister-in-law. More hot water is poured: our small cups are full.

"I'm really hungry," Grandmother calls out again.

Kayuko says: "She does that. She yells all the time. She doesn't mean to. It's just how she is."

The mood changes and Kayuko speaks quietly: "We lost our house and all our machines, and everything was covered in four feet of mud, so we can't be rice farmers anymore. Now Kazuyoshi works and I grow vegetables. Once a week I deliver them to the grocery store on my bicycle. We tried to plant at the old place, but no matter how deeply we dug in the old rice field, we still found debris. It scares me to think of what we might find. And we are afraid the tsunami will come again.

"I rented a plot from my uncle above the river. I'm growing radishes, eggplant, and arugula. But growing vegetables on someone else's land isn't the same. Kazuyoshi and I think of starting fresh, but we don't know where. Anyway, there's a rumor that there's a ghost roaming around Idohama, near Grandma's washed-away house. In the night you can see it. When we told Grandma about it she said she was scared. Now she says she doesn't believe in ghosts.

"I grew up near here in a big farmer's house. I didn't apply for temporary housing. I want to settle down. That's why we're here. I don't care that the government isn't paying. We just need to be settled. Sometimes I'm angry at people who are trying to get more than they deserve from the government. So many suffered and need money. If I went to them and said I had six family members, I could get three houses, three televisions, three refrigerators, three air conditioners. Some people are doing that, but I don't like it. It's wrong. I feel my one treasure is to help those who helped me."

Grandma yells: "What are you eating? I'm so hungry!"

Kayuko: "The tsunami has huge power to take things from people. It's different between those who don't have a house and those who do. We will never be the same as they are. To be honest, I don't know what I want or need. I don't want to live anymore. I feel hopeless. I'm doing every day the living-things that I have to do . . . but . . . it's not enough. We are talking about building a house. House is garbage. I've seen so many things turned to garbage, I don't want a new house, because the tsunami will happen again."

Masumi goes to her grandmother's side. They talk in hoarse whispers. Masumi tells her that she has been fed dinner. Grandmother protests: "I'm still hungry." Masumi unwraps a tiny piece of chocolate from her purse and puts it on Grandmother's tongue. "Just let it melt there," she says. Grandmother smiles and sucks the chocolate down.

Kayuko puts four more cookies by our teacups. "Ideally I'd like to have a small house with a garden plot in front, but I don't know if that's possible. Young people don't understand: I have to do whatever Kazuyoshi decides. He is the head of the family. Maybe I'm too negative, but to pretend to be happy is too hard. I think Kazuyoshi feels the same way. It's behind his happiness."

Kayuko's hands are big-knuckled and she holds them in the air when she's listening or trying to say something for which she has no words. "It's hard for me to express myself," she says, squinting and laughing. "If Kazuyoshi was here he'd talk more—but it is good he's not. I've said things that may be too negative."

When the door opens and Kazuyoshi bursts in, Kayuko's beautiful smile freezes. She goes silent. When she lived with the extended family she was treated in a traditional way—as a servant. She worked the land and did household chores, but was not allowed to eat at the table with the others. Now, husband and wife sit together at the low table. She looks at him expectantly, but there are no jokes tonight, no sharing of peanuts, no opening of beer after beer. He talks of his short-term government job cleaning debris. "It's hard. The heat goes up and down and wearing a helmet makes it hotter. The tsunami took all the trees; there is no shade."

His eyes narrow and he rubs his stomach. The work, he says, makes him dizzy and sick to his stomach. The debris is toxic and he's suffered several times from heat exhaustion. It's been 90 to 100 degrees. To relax, he goes to the public bathhouse with friends, drinks beer, and eats dinner because Kayuko rarely cooks. She never learned how. She worked the land and her mother cooked the meals.

Tonight, Kazuyoshi says he only wants to sleep. Like all Tohoku survivors, he and Kayuko are internal exiles. Their traditional loyalty to family and place works for them: they know how to make do in a cooperative way, yet they have no land on which to enact their obligations. The geographical constraints of island life can further go against them: it makes it almost impossible to move away. Social and religious traditions here keep families place-bound, as if those ideas about how and where to live had been shaped by the landscape.

We stand to leave. Many bows, smiles, promises of return visits, and questions about Kazuyoshi's Ping-Pong championship later, we find our shoes and step backwards out the door. At the last moment Kayuko thrusts a bag filled with eggplant, cucumbers, tomatoes, and green onions—vegetables she's grown on her rented patch of ground—into Kazuko's hands. As always, giving more than they receive.

Great-Uncle Satoru and Great-Aunt Satsuko

Kazuko buys a dozen donuts and we drive to the hated temporary apartment where Great-Uncle Satoru lives. We find him sitting on the floor in a small room with pale green walls and cheap tatami, surrounded by flower catalogues opened to pages of ranunculus, tulips, narcissus, daisies, lilies, peonies, and chrysanthemums. Instead of despairing, he's smiling. His wife brings tea. Great-Uncle Satoru picks out his favorite cream-filled donut and wipes the sides of his mouth as he eats, his appetite still voracious after months of sparse food.

When the donut is gone he looks up: "Today I was very bored, very angry at the government, so I went through my old mail because it was raining and there was nothing else to do. I opened a letter from city hall. I thought it was an announcement for another meeting about whether we could rebuild our houses or not, and do you know what the letter said?" We shook our heads no. "It said YES, we can fix up our houses and live there!"

Tears of joy flow. Great-Uncle Satoru keeps talking: "We have to understand that the area might have another tsunami, but as long as we understand the danger, the government can't force us to move. We can stay!"

He tells us he has already called the carpenter to start work on the house, and shows us a handful of nursery catalogues: "I've ordered seventy kinds of flowers! Just this morning! I want to plant lots of stuff! I don't care that flowers don't make money. I think people coming to the house and seeing all these plants will be a little happier. At least no one will get worse by seeing them.

Maybe they will think that there aren't so many bad people in the world after all."

He puts his hand to his bent-in-half back: "I've had trouble with my back for a long time. The walking stick that I could make longer or shorter got washed away. It's hard to walk, but planting flowers is okay because I'm bent over anyway!" he says, laughing.

The last donut is eaten, chocolate and crème dripping down the sides of his mouth while he shows us the ten varieties of tulips he's picked out: pink fringed, pure white, yellow and black striped, and a purple so dark it's almost black. Licking the last crumbs from his lips, he straightens up and smiles. "I want to celebrate New Year's in my own house. The carpenter says he will try to get it rebuilt in time. Once my house is fixed there will be plenty of vegetables and the flowers will already be in bloom. There will be food and you are all welcome! Please come!"

Typhoon, or an Ocean of the Streams of Story

Kazuko's feet itch—the big toes, the bottoms, and the backs of her heels—which means there'll be a big earthquake. Every day I've been here so far, there has been a tremor. But that's not at the head of the list of worries. Instead of autumn moon-viewing, we're ducking an oncoming typhoon.

Something has stopped breathing. There is no wind. Night touches its gray cloud-horns to our shoulders, our thick eyelids. Darkness hovers at the edge of Tohoku, then rears up and descends softly, its black wave unfolding into the hearts of erased towns.

Near morning the earthquake comes. I sleep through the first jolts, then jump, half-awake, and run into the hall. Dry words come into my mouth. *Where have they been stacking the dead?*

Downstairs we stare at the morning television news. The earthquake was a magnitude 6.8. More aftershocks come up through the living room floor. The weather map shows a force 7 typhoon approaching. "They usually go around to the west coast," Masumi says. "But this one is coming straight at us."

Still out in the Pacific, its probable course is marked by a red line, a red thread that will pull it overland near Nara, then through Tokyo, where it is predicted to veer straight north toward the Sendai Plain.

In advance of the storm, evacuations are taking place: 103,000 from Yokohama, 6,800 from Ishinomaki, 731 from Kesennuma. Outside the approaching storm drives a cool wedge into summer's furious heat. The sky thickens as if a bolt of gray velvet had been dropped into the middle of the street. Feeling unwell, I go upstairs. The air currents are braided: hot and wet with cool. A strong southerly pours embalming fluid around me. I lie sweating in solitude.

I have a fever and it's hard to keep track of what's moving and what's not: futon or cloud, storm or dream? My hair is wet, my head is dripping as if I'd been plunged under water; I think of Kikuchi-san who swam in tsunami waters and lived . . . I think of the streams of his story.

My fever spikes and drops. The heated core of the typhoon's gyrating center shakes from the Pacific Ocean to the coast of Honshu. Deepening convective bands wrap into a ragged eye. Mist falls into sacred mountains and hides there. By evening, temperatures have dropped thirteen degrees. The eye of the storm is now twelve miles wide; winds have accelerated to 100–120 miles per hour. The stiff-fronted tuxedos of black and white clouds roar north.

Tokyo's subways are shut down, as are the Shinkansen lines and all local trains and buses. People who can, walk home, but find they don't know the way on foot. They've never seen their neighborhoods from aboveground. A tree falls onto the front seat of a taxi. Narita airport closes; highways are flooded and bridges break in half. A man is found floating on a piece of plywood going out to sea and is rescued. Winds howl through Shinjuku at 102 miles per hour. The lights go out in Shizuoka. The storm is fast-moving, an ocean of wind and rain whirling at us in round waves. Streams of the life-and-death Tohoku stories I've heard will get soaked again. Full immersion. On the weather news the typhoon is shown as a red propeller spinning toward Sendai.

It's been dark for a long time. The mangled edge of the storm advances, its fringed tip like the tulips Great-Uncle Satoru ordered. Rain started Monday; now it's Thursday, and rain continues to fall hard. In the afternoon the typhoon hits the Fukushima Daiichi nuclear plant, causing a closed-circuit camera to stop, raising fears that there will be another hydrogen explosion, and that contaminated water will spread. TEPCO says no damage occurred, but who can believe them?

In the mountains landslides crush houses. A nine-year-old boy and his eighty-four-year-old friend, whose hand he was holding, are swept into a river. It's 7:30 p.m. The typhoon's center will pass Sendai in a few hours, exactly at high tide. The areas with the most coastal subsidence have been closed to traffic: Higashi-Matsushima, Shiogama, and fourteen areas of Ishinomaki. More residents are evacuated from the temporary houses into which they just moved.

Here on the western outskirts of Sendai, the windows of the house shake. We peer out. There's nothing to see but a glistening curtain; nothing to hear but a constant roar. Roads have become rivers, and ocean waters inundate land that has not dried since the coastal shelf changed shape, lifted, and dropped. I hear grinding: raucous winds pulverize tsunami debris into even smaller bits. The middle of the typhoon is upon us.

A tremor brings me to the edge of sleep, but it is silence that wakes me. Typhoon 16 has passed north. Behind it, the whole world is blue. A storm is inebriation, and so is a fever. Mind and weather mix. A cyclonic wind spirals inside the throat. Time loses its way. At the coast, surf plunges, collapses, spills, and surges. Foamy crests and smooth tunnels unspool. The evacuation count, including the ruined coast of Tohoku, has reached over 341,000.

I think of the typhoon as an aerial ocean—a single organism that hovers over us as if from a remembered thirst. I drink cold tea and bottled water. The weather channel's red propeller spins toward Hokkaido.

* * *

Here, the Earth-altar breaks.
We've always been on the move.
Past and future—those are places
I've never reached.
Where the tsunami wave came and went,
that's where I am.

Hirayama's Blog

Almost September.

Flooding at Kuwagasaki from the spring tide. Because the ground sank 50 cm, many parts of the area are submerged. And this on a clear day. Imagine what it will be like if the typhoon strikes here.

September 1

Still worried as the typhoon approaches. If any waves come in, no boat will be able to stay in the Miyako port.

We received some saury fish today from the boats that unloaded their catch for the second time since March. Delicious! Virtually all the saury boats from here were washed away.

September 3

Found my ship's flag hanging from the side of my son's school building. Thank you to whoever picked it up and saved it. I think I'll donate it to the school. Grass is growing over our old house site. This town may never be back to what it was.

September 11

My kids and I took a walk from the house to look at Kuwagasaki, our part of town. Nothing has changed. Time has stopped and the wounds of our hearts have not healed. We will be victims for a much longer time. The houses and debris have been cleaned up, but nothing else since then. The ground-works are still left behind. A bridge can be seen still broken in half.

This was the first time to take the kids with me to Kuwaga-saki. My daughter used to say she didn't want to see the broken houses, but today she seemed different. Weeds covering where the buildings used to be. Vegetables and flowers also growing. Tomatoes, cucumbers, pumpkin . . . My daughter seemed to enjoy picking the flowers.

Not a soul in sight as we walk around. My son said, "Dad, this town is finished. We have to get out of here." He took me by surprise. He is still a child, but spoke such serious words. Wondering about the state of his heart shocked me

Even with people from Miyako—depending upon whether they were affected by the tsunami or not—you can tell there is a difference between us.

We're supposed to stay in our temporary houses for 2 years, but there are a lot of worries for our future. First, securing our next home. Is it going to be an apartment or rented house, or government housing? I don't think there will be any openings 2 years from now. Frankly, I don't think it's possible. People living in temporary houses in Taro and Yamada have similar fears. If all the people rush into Miyako, there will be no vacancies left. No place to go. Since March, there has been a constant outflow of people leaving the disaster areas. Younger generations seek new opportunities in a new place. Such is reality.

Considering our future, leaving town may not be an option. But if younger people leave, the towns will not develop, and those who are left will have to work hard to amend that loss.

September 14

The sea wind in Sanriku was good today with a fast tide. Twenty-two Celsius in the water. Good thing there is no wind, but instead, a light shower. I tried to trawl with a net to find the tools that got cut off and washed away. They were washed toward land, and it took me 2 hours to find them. Debris had tangled in the rope and it was a mission to get it off. There was a lot of strain on the lines too. When out fishing, if the line ever gets tied up around you, then you are a dead man, dragged to the bottom of the ocean. Strictly speaking, this is an extremely dangerous job with death on your mind constantly. It wears you down. You just think, "I'm going to die. I'm going to die." If the line gets caught around your arm, the flesh will be torn off and you'll be left with the bone sticking out. The oil pressure line wheeler got stuck from the weight of the debris and made a terrible noise. "I don't want to die" constantly pops into my head during cleanup. Times like these I wish I wasn't a fisherman.

September 19

It's much colder today than yesterday. Lowest was 15°C, too cold for short sleeves and sleeping with opened windows. It dropped from 30°C yesterday; today's highest was 19°C. Rained today with strong winds.

With fall and winter approaching, I worry about the living conditions in the temporary housing. Especially older people living alone. There are many 65+ year old people who have been affected by the disaster. As days go by, they may need aid. There's a person over 80, and I went to see if he was okay. After the Kobe earthquake, there were stories about lonely deaths inside the temp houses, and I worry that this will happen here. I feel that the bond, the ties and communication between survivors, has grown weaker. It was better when we were living in the evacuation centers. Winter is coming. Living in temporary housing may be very severe for us.

September 21

8:00 p.m. Typhoon coming up the coast. On the boat now. High tide was at 7 p.m. so we came to deal with it. The water is right up at the top of the seawall. Because there aren't many waves, it hasn't gone over the wall, but the wind and rain are getting stronger. I have to protect my boat so I'll be working through the night. The pressure is getting to my nerves. So worried . . . If the Hei River increases, the boat will be in severe danger. This is grinding me down. My stomach aches from stress. Have to keep this up until morning.

After the Typhoon

Seventeen inches of rain have fallen. Here at the coast, there's no difference between river and field, tree and ocean. Timber from the mountains floats downstream; trees spear oncoming waves. A dark mirror shatters where an egret lands, shadow-first, on water, its feet slamming down, causing light to scatter, spread and dissipate. A sultry stillness hardens.

Masumi, Kazuko, and I drive as far as possible, but have to stop where the water comes in through the doors. We back up and try another route. The whole quake-dropped coast is inundated. Newly planted seedlings are bent down by heavy rainwater, if they can be seen at all. The small channelized river that divided Great-Uncle Satoru's land from Grandmother's land has risen over its banks and is now a single body of water that extends to the sea. Water comes up to the open veranda of Great-Uncle's house. The garden they just planted is gone. Will they survive the shock of losing it all again? Will the government still let them rebuild?

We tromp through shin-deep water. The first floors of damaged houses that had just been repaired are wet and water-stained. Rice fields are holding ponds, tile roofs that had not been fixed have exposed the interiors of standing houses to the typhoon. No one is around. "I'm glad you can see it this way. This is how it looked right after the tsunami," Masumi says.

I'm looking at fiction; I'm looking at truth; my eyes are wet from the downpour.

* * *

Our plan was to drive all the way north to Kamaishi and Miyako today to see Kikuchi-san, "the Swimmer," then north to visit Hirayama-san and his father. When we call, they all say, please don't come. You won't be able to get through. We try anyway. At the least, we could make it to Shichigahama, to the Buddhist temple, Ikoji, but a policeman stops us and tells us to turn around. Did the beautiful new temple, rebuilt by the Akita carpenters, survive? We call but can't get through.

We pass the white elementary school where Masumi's aunt and uncle—Kazuyoshi and Kayuko—almost drowned, its first two floors still in ruins. Nearby, a graveyard is in disrepair—all the gravestones toppled. Anything that was reclaimed, replanted, or rebuilt has been undone, and the rainwater is toxic: falling water and falling leaves carry increased amounts of cesium-137. Workers have been struggling in vain to decontaminate soil.

"I grew up around here. There used to be houses, shops, and temples. Now they are gone; I thought they would have been rebuilt by now, but even if they had, they would be covered by water again," Masumi says. "It feels so strange."

At the grocery store, Kazuko buys yellow and orange flowers. Tomorrow, September 23, is Ohigan, the autumnal equinox, the day when flowers are put on ancestral graves.

The government is threatening to exterminate animals left behind in the twenty-kilometer zone, even though they can easily be cared for by willing animal rescue groups. TEPCO claims that the power plant withstood the quake, though workers inside the plant claim the opposite is true. Polluted water that had been used to cool the reactors at Fukushima Daiichi continues to leak into the sea.

A Japanese husband and wife have become self-styled animal

rescue guerrillas, defying authorities, evading police roadblocks, and going into the radioactive zone to rescue dogs. Great-Uncle Satoru's hope darkens, as if hope itself was tenebrific, the cause of night. His flooded winter vegetables will not come into being.

The typhoon veered east of Miyako, sparing the fishing boats of Hirayama and his father. The last of three Hana Fuda cards for September bear the image of a chrysanthemum, but with a full cup of sake.

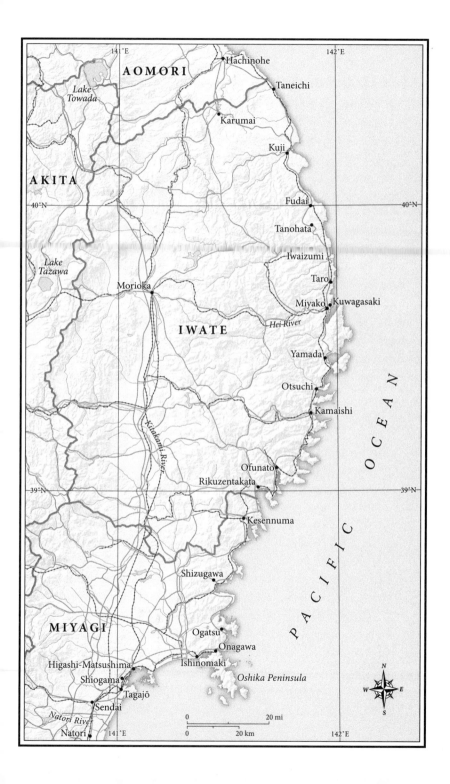

Hirayama's Blog

September
  Miyako weather is fine since the early hours. The typhoon avoided us. We were lucky this time. It didn't hit us. Kamagasaki, the destroyed town near the port, is quiet. The word "rebuilding" gets tossed around, but it's all talk and nothing has been done. Miyako is the same—comparing the affected and nonaffected areas—the affected areas have been left behind in time. But that's the reality. Going home now. Ocean too rough. Father and I will make buoys today.

* * *

Month's end—no moon.
A storm embraces
thousand-year cedars.
—MATSUO BASHŌ

Floating Island and the Fukushima 50

I tell Kazuko about the dessert my mother always made at Christmas called Floating Island—a dab of meringue floating on a sea of custard.

Fukushima Daiichi is another kind of island, a radioactive wound surrounded by ghost towns—places that have been evacuated and may never be inhabited again. The nuclear power plant continues to be a hotspot and what has been called "a fortress of sacrifice and duty."

When TEPCO called for volunteers to come and work there, offers rolled in—too many of them. Men in their fifties called first, including a fifty-nine-year-old a few months from retirement. They were trying to take up the jobs in order to spare younger men from being exposed to serious amounts of contamination.

The Fukushima 50 have been compared to the 47 Ronin (lordless, wandering samurai in feudal Japan), their work at Daiichi feeding on the spirit of Bushido, the warrior's way, where loyalty, sacrifice, persistence, and honor are upheld. They are also the "new *hibakusha*," and will be held at arm's length by others, much as the 1945 survivors of Hiroshima and Nagasaki were. Young men will not be able to marry, for fear that they will become sick and unable to provide for a family. Older men will be on the lookout for cancer to carry them away soon.

Masao Yoshida, the fifty-six-year-old Daiichi manager who ignored TEPCO's on-and-off-again order to stop pumping seawater into a reactor and by doing so saved many lives, was hospitalized on November 24. He'd worked for nine months to bring Daiichi under control and was the leader of the Fukushima 50. He's been diagnosed with esophageal cancer.

Just before I leave for the airport, we spend an hour at the graveyard where Kazuko's ancestors are buried. Rain comes in fits and starts. Incense is lit. Clumps of bamboo encircle us, their hollow trunks knocking out a spare song. Wind pushes the wet remnants of the typhoon eastward. The sky goes dark, then bright. It's autumn. Wind sweeps it. Clouds crumble. Leaf is nothing.

December

December

The Dark gives the Light a place to shine.

LAO TZU, *Taoteching*,
TRANSLATED BY RED PINE

It is dark when I wake, and dark by midafternoon. Today, December 8, is Rohatsu, the day the Buddha attained nirvana. When I ask American friends who are monks what they will do this day, one says, "We will sit in meditation." Another says, "We will cook feast food." A third says: "I can't remember. Anyway, we practice meditation because we *are* enlightened; we don't practice to *become* enlightened."

Driving to the airport from home to catch a flight to Tokyo, the BBC World News is on, and a professor mentions the Shinto creation myth: "Brother and Sister had sex and gave birth to islands. Then they got lonely and gave birth again. From the left eye came the Sun goddess, and from the right, the god of the Moon."

Strapped in for fourteen hours, we bend under the fractured arm of Alaska, as moon cuts ice into facets and snow clouds mound up high enough to touch the plane's wings. From the Aleutians, we arrow south past Kamchatka, the Kurile Islands, the tentacle-armed shores of Hokkaido, and follow the undulant edge of the Pacific to touch down, mid-Honshu.

Nikki calls: "Ahoy, Gretel, welcome back, check out the lunar eclipse!" I crane my head to see: a sleeve of ember-reddened darkness slides over the moon. When I return to Tohoku, I will reenter the umbra. All paths are made of shadow and substance. As Lao Tzu says, darkness gives the light a place to shine.

Now the moon's shadow slides, illuminating a path, a *michi*, and I follow it. I go south instead of north, to Nara, to visit old friends, the writer Pico Iyer and his wife, Hiroko.

It's said in Japan that drinking tea together constitutes an act of peace. At the Nara Hotel, an oddly shaped teapot is laid on its side and said to be "sleeping." Pico and I watch it, as if watching a child. It doesn't move. We talk quietly. I hear faint music. In the adjoining room there's a photograph of Albert Einstein playing the piano at this hotel, where the Dalai Lama also likes to stay.

We mull over the Buddhist law of "the truth of suffering." To say that the tsunami survivors' attitude toward their tremendous loss is stoicism would be to underestimate the complexity of their response. Courage and self-discipline are evident everywhere in this deeply traditional culture, as well as an ability to accept "what is" without sentimentality, even as the government persists with its numbing denials. But the pain of loss is staggering; there's confusion, nightmarish fear, and there are suicides.

Pico says, "For all the sadness that will not go away, I can't help feeling, after twenty years living in Japan, that it's the country's strengths, more than its weaknesses, that have been and will be highlighted by the recent cataclysms."

In the dark we walk through the Deer Park on our way to dinner. The moon shines through jagged pines. A deer brushes under a branch: brown needles fall. Nara, the first permanent capital of Japan and center of Buddhism, reeks of *furui*—a feeling of being old, yet burnished, like the shaved head of a monk pushing through delusion. We agree that the tsunami teaches us to "un-ask" the usual questions: Why me? Why these losses, this suffering? People here don't make an enemy of sorrow.

They know that pain is real; that neurotic suffering is only the flapping of ego. Happiness is allowed to free-fall through grief's fetters. The one never precludes the other.

Shunyata means being "empty of self," and therefore able to take in whatever happens. That's what I see going on here—shock and disbelief, acceptance, survivor's euphoria, deep sadness, and then movement: life's extraordinary experiences entwined with the ordinary, and from that littered ground, the courage to leap.

Pico's wife, Hiroko, meets us at a traditional, unlit restaurant. "Dark magic still happens here. Believe it," she says. We laugh hard—so happy to be together again.

"My grandfather came from priest-side; my grandma from spirit-side," Hiroko says. Plates of food come. "Both had powers. My grandmother saw a Fox Woman, a fox who pretended to be a human being. Another time she saw a thief running away with someone's money, and my grandfather cast a spell on him so he couldn't move. If we don't have rain, we still go to the mountain where the dragon-god lives and offer food. In the old days, women were sacrificed. Not now, though." Laughter. "Pretty soon, it is the Year of the Dragon!"

She leans across the deeply shadowed table and whispers: "I know when ghosts are around. I'm scared to meet them. Sometimes the spirit comes at midnight. Behind me, a feeling [*she gestures with her hand*], so I step aside and let them go by." As with the nation's sorrow.

In a phone call on the train the next day, heading toward Sendai, Masumi tells me it won't be possible to visit her aunts and uncles. "Please understand, they are having a bad time now," she says. In an inexplicable reversal, Great-Uncle Satoru canceled the carpenter whom he had hired to rebuild his house. He says he is confused about what to do. Yet he takes a taxi from his temporary apartment to his old house to replant the vegetables that were destroyed by the typhoon. And the flower seeds have begun to arrive by the hundreds.

Kazuyoshi and Kayuko, Masumi's uncle and aunt, have returned to the neighborhood as well, planting vegetables in front of where Grandmother's house once stood. Their neighborhood group is still trying to decide which piece of land offered by the government to buy. But so far, no land is suitable.

"If we ask Kazuyoshi and Kayuko about it now, they'll feel they have to give an answer, even if it's not true, so better not to," Masumi says.

The tick of railroad tracks is a clock summoning the winter season; its rhythm, a reminder of the episodic taking of towns by the wave. Moon after moon lights up the ocean's destruction. The yen surges and gold drops. Night is bright. Moon has shed its embers. Cesium-137 is found in baby formula. Money for tsunami survivors has been used to help prop up the Japanese whaling industry. The Daiichi nuclear plant scraps plans to dump its contaminated water into the ocean. TEPCO'S new insurance policy costs three hundred million yen a year.

It's revealed that eight and a half tons of radioactive water have leaked from reactor 4, whose structural integrity has become worrisome. Experts say that a collapse of its spent fuel rods could cause a disaster worse than the three reactor meltdowns. The first load of contaminated debris from Tohoku is shipped out to be buried somewhere near Yokohama. A total of "thirty-three football stadiums'" worth of dirt still needs to find a home. Older couples from Fukushima Prefecture are taking the train to Yamagata to get away from the radiation, but once there, commit suicide because they can't stand to be away from their old neighborhoods.

* * *

At a small station north of Sendai, Nikki, Abyss-san, and I meet up once again. Abyss-san buys vegetables at the station store, then we drive north. His mountain house is frigid inside, but swept clean. In the morning we drive toward the walled fishing town of Miyako. *Unwalled* is a better word. Water gates are still bent as if made of aluminum foil, and seawalls are breached and broken. We roll by a vacant lot where cranes and front-end loaders are being rented. Salmon season has just ended: their eviscerated bodies hang to dry from the eaves of every house, the sides held open with three inch long sticks.

Death leaves marks: a woman told Abyss-san that her fourteen-year-old grandchild was practicing with the school's swim team when the tsunami occurred. The wave came over the pool. The granddaughter survived but she had scratch marks all down her legs made by other girls as they tried to claw their way up to air. They drowned.

Back at the mountain house the tiny bush warblers chatter, but no longer sing.

Miyako

Midday and Miyako harbor is lively. The fish market, a huge structure where fish of all kinds are unloaded, washed, sorted, iced, and stored, has a new roof and three walls. Seventy-five-foot trawlers with purple bows are lined up at the dock, and deckhands are unloading debris they've disentangled from the nets. Their catch of saury is already being readied for sale. Since the ice factory began working again, there is no limit to the number of fish brought in.

Today Hirayama-san and his father are working on the far side of the bay. They've already rebuilt their tool and storage shed and are making buoys for clam season. They work together in silent, choreographic unison—braiding back rope ends, securing nets, tying knots.

"When we saw you last time we were living in a shelter," Hirayama-san, the thirty-six-year-old son, begins. His name means "flat mountain," but he's anything but flat. Tall and lithe, he's pencil-thin with a youthful face, and like his father, has a calm, straightforward demeanor. "Now we're in temporary housing up on the hill. It's tough—it's very cramped, especially with small children, but it's better than the shelter. We have a different pattern than other people: we go to bed at 5:00 p.m. and get up at midnight to go fishing. When we were going to bed, everyone else was just relaxing, having dinner. It was hard to sleep in a room full of people.

"Once we moved to temp housing, we had to begin to pay for everything ourselves. The government gave us three payments per household: an initial 500,000 yen, then 800,000, then 100,000 for living costs. Now that's finished and we're on our own. In two years, we're supposed to move on, but how and where, I don't know."

Father: We used to live in a big house. At least our electric use and bills are smaller now! We want to get out of the temporary housing, but there's nowhere to go. It may be five or six years before we can move . . .

Things are hard for office workers and those who have no job at all. Recently, in Morioka, a pile of donated clothes and food was incinerated because they were no longer needed in that city (which was unaffected by the tsunami). But there are many needs here. They didn't consider others. The official who ordered the burning was punished.

The government is now giving aid to construction companies so they can stay in business, but our payments have ended. If we work hard and make money we'll be able to rebuild.

Hirayama-san: I started writing a blog as a hobby. I've been doing it for three or four years as a way to talk to friends. But it got more intense after the tsunami. In the first few days I got one hundred thousand visitors, then two hundred thousand. People wanted to know what had happened here. We had no cell phone service, but I could upload from my phone. We only had power a few hours during the day so I used it to send text and photos.

Hirayama's father smiles. He's almost sixty-nine, but his face is unlined and he's still handsome. His talk is by turns untroubled, cheerful, and earnest. He's matter-of-fact but never bitter.

Father: I don't get anything about the Internet. Or blogs. I can't even use a cell phone. Anything Western or electronic—

I'm lost! The tracking devices on our trawlers used to be in Japanese. Now they're all in English, Katakana, borrow-words. Why? When I was young people lived more closely. We'd go down to the port and talk all together, exchange information about fish and the weather. No one does that much anymore. But the scale of this disaster was huge. It didn't matter if you had a cell phone or not. No one knew where anyone was, or if they were alive.

I've been here all my life. There have been no large-scale tsunamis. In 1963, when the urchin cages started popping up on the surface of the water after a *jishin,* I knew there would be a tsunami, but the wave was small. But before I was born, there were tsunami two times, and twice, the family houses were washed away. My grandmother was caught by the wave and swam to safety in 1933. Her house was fifty meters from where our house was . . . both have been swept away by a wave. We have this kind of loss in our family memory, and yet, we continue to live close to the ocean! Many people swam and survived in this tsunami too.

About twenty fishing trawlers went out when the Wave was coming in. It was a giant wall of water, but it's what we know how to do. The motorway was closed, so many fishermen couldn't get to their boats in time. We were lucky. But once out there, when we borrowed some binoculars and looked, we could see everything was gone—our houses, our shed—and we were afraid to go back in. We stayed out for two days.

There will be another tsunami. We always have an escape plan in mind. There's a lot of tectonic plate pressure in the Sanriku area up here in the north. So in the next thirty years, another 9.0 quake could result from seismic movement. Our peninsula faces north, so we'll get hit by it. Those of us who lost houses must move from the neighborhood where our family has lived for many generations. It's hard to think of it, but we will.

Hirayama-san: The disaster has been hard on young children. My five-year-old gets scared every time there's a shake. She won't stay in a room by herself. There always has to be a parent or grandparent with her. It's hard to believe, but the Wave that came into our town was more than 124 feet high! It crashed over the seawall, smashed the water gates, inundated the fish market roof and the four-story building next to it. I instruct my children in *tendenko*—it means don't go back for anything, don't spend time trying to save others' lives. Just run to high ground. That's what I drill into them.

Some people didn't see the water coming. There were houses in the way, and they couldn't see it. They thought they were okay. But a woman high up in a building was yelling down to them to run. Some heard her and ran. My grandmother didn't want to leave the house. She said she didn't care if she died. But we cared. They had to slap her face and drag her to safety.

Tsunamis are cruel. Some are victimized, others are not. I keep my important papers with me at all times. If the fishery here dies out, the whole town dies. All the fishermen are working hard to keep it going.

Father: We lost everything except our boat, but we still have our lives. We can't do anything about possessions. We knew a tsunami would come sometime. When we were coming in on our boat and couldn't see any houses here, we knew it was all gone.

It's better to look into the future. We're grateful to strangers and distant relatives who gave kindness and aid, to you for coming from so far away to see us again. Our family has everything we need. Others need more help than we do. Some kids lost their parents. Wives lost husbands. Grandparents are raising their children's kids. One man lost his two children, his wife, and his parents. Now he wonders how he can keep living.

A bank of clouds lies on the horizon in the west where the sun begins to sink. Father and son finish the last buoy, working seamlessly and in unison, never having to speak about what they've been doing with their hands. I take out my camera and snap a picture. Hirayama-san is tall. The father is shorter and strong. Both men look younger than they are, fit in body and mind.

Dark comes at a little past four in the afternoon. The air is crisp. They close up their shed to go home for dinner. His hands finally at rest, the father turns to me:

"In the end, it's important to have the mental will and physical strength to keep going. There's still so much to clean up, so much debris in the ocean that gets caught in our nets. One fisherman trolled up a bag with 10 million yen inside. He donated it to aid relief."

I ask him if he still believes in hope. "Hope?" he says, then grins. There's a long silence. He straightens up and looks at the sky as if making a wish. "My one hope is to build a house on a hill, on high ground."

Abyss-san's Mountain Home

A gray cloud in the shape of an eyebrow cuts the gibbous moon's oblong top. No sign of last week's eclipse. Now I wonder if the burnt part, the first part of the moon to go black, hasn't been lopped off and flung somewhere. The van chugs up the mountain. We pass a car-killed deer dragged to the side of the road, being eaten by hawks, then the stone gate that leads to a hidden shrine an hour's walk up the hill. The steps are green moss; the air at $-5\,°C$ is chilly; the hydrangeas by the side of the road have lost their blue.

Even unseen, the Pacific Ocean is present. It's a double-jointed shoulder that keeps lunging at this coast, bigger, at 64.1 million square miles, than any landmass. I think of those who drowned, the horizon vanishing, the mind no longer able to track the grand and small movements of life. In their last look, what did they see? Perhaps sky was all that was left, the slate on which transience is written: cloud, rain, snow, wind, sun . . . *kumo, ame, yuki, kaze, taiyo.* In Japan, the words for rain change according to season and location.

"I keep working to pay my respects to those who lost their lives," Abyss-san says again.

* * *

From the *OED*: *Abyss,* "the primal chaos, bowels of the earth, lower world," from the Greek *abussos,* "bottomless." Deep waves in abyssal life that ripple down the sides of underwater mountains, then crest and curl in events of chaotic turbulence.

Abyss-san insists, despite his mounting pessimism about life in Japan, that his name comes from Ebisu, the God of Happiness.

Ito-San, the Geisha

They sleep in bunk beds in a tiny room—the "last geisha of Kamaishi" and her middle aged architect nephew, Satoshi-san—because there is no room for two futons on the floor. It's a two-room "apartment," about 550 square feet, one of hundreds grouped in barrack-like rows.

The evacuation centers, found usually in school gyms such as the one where Ito-san and Satoshi-san lived after the disaster, are now closed, and those whose houses were washed away have no choice but to move into these cramped quarters.

I bang on the outer door and call to her: "*Gomen kudasai,* Ito-san . . . ?" No answer. I walk to the back of the apartment-barrack, but there are no doors. At the front again, I step through to the outer sliding door, remove shoes, enter the tiny space that serves as bathroom, laundry room and kitchen: "Ito-san!"

The television is on. Maybe she can't hear me. A few feet more, and another sliding door opens. I burst in, startling her, then hold out my arms to give her a hug.

When one comes into eighty-four-year-old Tsuyako Ito's presence, the world smooths out and gains an elegance missing elsewhere. Her lipstick is fresh and bright, her gray hair pulled back tight. Her high cheekbones are like arrows pointing toward the future. From the corner of the flat-screen TV (provided by the government in every temporary housing unit) a photograph of the empress sticks out from one side. "I share a birthday with the empress," Ito-san says. "It's December 23, though I'm eight years older than she is."

The day is cold and we sit on the floor at the *kotatsu,* a low table with a heated blanket over our crossed legs. "I lost many things, but I still have the words to the song," she says, eyes twinkling.

High up on the wall are framed photographs salvaged from her ruined house: of Satoshi-san, her nephew, who she says is down in Kyushu getting a bit of sun before starting his own architectural firm in the coming week. Another photograph is of friends at the Kamaishi restaurant where she performs, including a priest from Otsuchi who was washed away in the tsunami. There is a photograph of her performing in Tokyo, at thirty years old, with long black hair and an elaborately embroidered kimono. "I gave my good kimono away. Now I wish I still had it," she says a bit ruefully.

"I can't pay $5,000 for a kimono I won't wear very much longer," she says. "But the most important thing is to pass on the Kamaishi Hamauta before it is lost." She looks straight at me, takes my hand, and smiles: "I've found someone!" she says excitedly. "I've given the song to her." She hands me another photograph taken in the evacuation center where I first met her. "That's Megumi Kimura, a geisha from Tokyo. In July, she came here and I taught her the Hamauta, the Bay Song."

It's unusual for geishas to stray from their local towns. Each region of Japan holds on to its own traditional acts, and they are never passed from one region to another, much less from one province to another. But the March disaster changed protocol and erased territorial boundaries. Even the emperor and empress made their way north to Kamaishi, and Megumi-san did the same. Upon reading in a newspaper that Ito-san had lost everything, the forty-nine-year-old geisha came to Kamaishi bearing a gift: a new shamisen.

Ito-san unwrapped the instrument, tuned it, and immediately played the old song for the visiting geisha. She asked Megumi-san if she would learn it and pass it on. "We had the first lesson here in the shelter," Ito-san said. "The people at the gym got to see a real geisha rehearsal."

When Megumi-san returned to Tokyo she taught the Hamauta to her four apprentices. "Even though the girls aren't from here, at least the song will be carried on," Ito-san says. "And maybe they could come up here sometime and perform for the people here. As long as someone owns it, it can't be stolen, or forgotten. I'm so grateful," she says.

First the shamisen, then a kimono. "I don't need anything else now," she says. In August, and again in October, Ito-san took the Shinkansen to Tokyo, where she and Megumi-san performed the Hamauta together. "Not only was the white geisha there, the one you met here from Australia, but also, a geisha from Shinagawa who was actually a man!

"I hadn't been onstage for a long time, since before the tsunami, but I wasn't nervous," she said, her eyes twinkling. "I just pulled on my kimono and went out there and sang."

Last week, the owners of Saiwairou, the Kamaishi restaurant, asked her to return. They are through hosting funeral dinners. "Many of my friends were there. Almost like old times, except for those who were taken by the Wave."

There's a long silence, then: "Everything has to come to an end sometime," she says. A geisha's sense of beauty also stands for self-discipline and endurance. "I'll keep performing the song until I'm at 'the rice age'—eighty-eight, the last celebrated year before I reach one hundred," she explains. "When I turn eighty-eight, I'll step off the stage. I hope to end my life then. That gives me three more years. It's a personal wish. There are no more geishas left in Kamaishi. In this town, the geisha tradition will end with me."

Ofunato

Reiko-san lives in a village on the far side of the port, so that most of the town of Ofunato is obscured from view. She's a friend of the American Buddhist nun Tenku Ruff, who asked that I pay a visit. As we drive the loop road it's easy to see how the Wave entered the harbor, then pushed out, claw-like, in all directions, lapping up villages in a wide swath, almost a full circle.

Reiko-san is in temporary housing, though she can barely manage to care for herself. She is so bent over with osteoporosis, she appears to have no torso at all. When we find her, she's perched on a bed—merely a head and legs. But her wide, sun-creased face is welcoming. She says that in eighty-six years, she's never once left her village.

"I didn't know my house had been washed away. They didn't tell me. They took me to the evacuation center, making sure they didn't pass my house so I wouldn't see. By the time they told me, it had been torn down. I didn't have a chance to get anything out of it. All I had was my handbag. My husband is in hospital. He's not well, not remembering me, so there was no one to help. All I could do was put my palms together," she says. She's a member of the local Buddhist temple, and a monk named Yuji, from a town in the mountains, visits three times a week and helps care for her.

"I was lured here by my husband fifty years ago, after the war. We were the first generation to live in Ofunato. We had a big house and I raised our children there. Now, they are in their sixties and their houses were washed away too.

"I never imagined it would happen in my lifetime. I'm eighty-three. Or is it eighty-six? I can't remember. There are signs in the village that show how high the water went in the previous tsunami. I remember it came in very slowly, but this time, the water came fast. It was a huge wave facing us. Some fishermen won't go back out to the ocean. They get seasick; they're too scared.

"The city provides lunch for me every day. My son is wealthy. He had a big statue of the Buddha. His house was at the highest point, way up on the hill, and even that was washed away! He tells my husband that our house is gone too, but he forgets and says, 'I want to go home.'

"I don't want to die before my husband but it's hard, not being able to walk. My only wish is for him to die in peace; then I can go as well." She begins crying. I take her hand in mine; Nikki takes the other. She wipes her tears, smiles a broad smile, and passes a box of *manju*—Japanese sweets.

"He was a hard worker. He harvested scallops and cared for us. He built our home. The hardest thing is to be separated from someone who is still here. Now we are poor. We have nothing. I really don't want to live anymore. Really, the truth is, I would like to put an end to my life soon."

Rikuzentakata

Evening. Because Abyss-san's house has no hot water, we stop at a workman's hotel up the hill from the devastated town of Rikuzentakata to use the public bath. In the steam, a naked middle-aged woman, one of the local workers, greets me in a loud, hoarse voice and shows me where to stow my clothes. Nikki and I sit on pink plastic stools, wash ourselves, then slide into hot water.

"The river is within us, the sea is all about us," a line from T. S. Eliot's poem "The Dry Salvages" begins. Radioactive water is absorbed by living tissue. We scrub dirt off, as radioactive iodine and cesium-137 soak in.

Fresh water pours from a pipe over Nikki's shoulder.

We cannot think of a time that is oceanless
Or of an ocean not littered with wastage
Or of a future that is not liable
Like the past, to have no destination . . .

Ten naked women's bodies stir around, old and young, the unbeautiful and the lithe, hands, wrists, breasts floating, minds unraveling, letting loose scraps of dreams and knife-sharp scenes of a water-flattened town. Seismic rumblings cause waves to travel across the bathwater. They bump into us, into our shoulders and cheeks like the abyssal waves that peel off underwater mountains, causing gentle crests to curl.

We drift. When the heat gets to be too much, we rise up, displacing water, as if our bodies had the kind of seismic power that could tear Earth apart. We sit on the edge cooling ourselves while Nikki tells how, when translating for London journalists from the *Telegraph* nine days after the disaster, they talked to a young boy, aged ten, who had been looking for his mother in the rubble of Rikuzentakata.

"The boy finally accepted that his mother was dead after three days, then went looking for her body at the temporary morgues, but never found her," she tells me. "His father turned out to be the town's mayor. When the tsunami came, Toba-san, the mayor, clung onto the roof of city hall as the third floor of the building, where the American schoolteacher, Monty Dickson, among others, thought he would be safe, was ravaged by a thirty-three-foot-high wave.

"Toba-san watched his own house torn apart by the Wave, knowing his wife was inside. But duty to the town came first, he explained: 'I'm a human being and a father . . . but I had to stay at the office . . . a lot of my staff have been lost or have lost their families too . . . ' "

Nikki tells me how the young boy's friend ran when he saw the water coming, leaving behind his own mother, who had gone back into the house for something; how other classmates were picked up by their mothers and never seen again.

We climb out of the bath, dry ourselves with tiny towels, and put on our dirty clothes again. Abyss-san emerges from the men's side and we rumble through the outskirts of this nonexistent town with the ghosts of its 12,449 dead, including the sixty-eight city officials, wandering legless around the moving van.

In June the survivors organized a traditional dance to commemorate those who died, held at one of the few remaining buildings, Kanogoji Temple, perched high on the hillside overlooking the ruins. Now, debris piles exhale smoke, and the single remaining pine out of thousands of trees has gained government protection as a symbol for the destruction here, and for survival.

Nine months earlier when I first saw this town, I was stunned by the extent of destruction. Now, passing through morning and evening, stopping for gas, groceries, and a dip in the public baths, the sight is almost commonplace. Is it possible to become inured to near-total destruction?

We no longer brood over the memory of the 284 firefighters who drowned while trying to close the water gates, or the deaths at city hall, or the lack of standing buildings, or the foaming ocean with its whitecaps' glinting brevity—not because we've become hardhearted, but perhaps the opposite: we've begun living the reality, dipping our own bodies into its toxic waters, no longer just voyeurs.

Up-mountain. The effect of the bath pushes me somewhere new. I can't think; the apparatus of logic fails me. My mind free-falls like a building uprooted, collapsing, floating . . . Once we make it to Abyss-san's house, I go to bed with all my clothes on, including hat and parka, intending to take just a short nap before dinner, and sleep until dawn.

* * *

Breakfast. "A long curry." That's what I call it, because the hot red curry Abyss-san made lasts all week and is our breakfast as well as our dinner. He announced to us when we arrived that he would no longer eat out at restaurants because they bought food from the cheapest sources, food grown in the highly radiated Fukushima Prefecture. At his mountain hideaway we drink hot tea made with Evian water and eat only vegetables and fruit grown in Hokkaido.

On January first, Wakamizu (*wake* = young; *mizu* = water), the first water drawn is said to have magical powers to maintain health and prolong life. But what of the waters of Fukushima, Miyagi, or Iwate? Will anyone drink it? In a bumptious effort to show how safe the new decontamination process at Daiichi is, a politician, Yasushiro Sonoda, drank a glass of water collected from the puddles under one of the damaged reactors at Daiichi.

Abyss-san lays the dosimeter on the ground by his stream. It reads 2.01 microseiverts. Not too bad, but not great. He looks up: "It's important that radiation readings continue and are publicized so that people know what to eat and drink and where to live."

In his unheated kitchen he cooks on a single gas burner. Every night we arrive back in the mountains exhausted and hungry. He heats up the huge pot of curry and we're grateful. The big *donburi* bowls in which it's served are frigid. We crouch together on the floor by the small woodstove; we use the outhouse, the toilet seat now wrapped with blue cloth to keep our bums warm. From that perch we track Orion's belt rising. Snow falls. Red curry heats us from the inside out. Burning logs warm our skin.

ABYSS-SAN'S CURRY RECIPE

Sauté cloves, bay leaves, fenugreek, chili peppers, cardamom,
   curry leaf, and garlic in mustard oil.
Add sliced onion, turmeric, coriander, and cumin.
Add chopped potatoes and carrots, then tomatoes.
Rinse China beans and lentils, then add in with salt.
Add enough water to cover. Cover and cook for one hour or
   more, or until beans are soft.
Make an equally large pot of rice with wheat berries.
Fry Aju hing seeds and add to the curry at the end. Serve.
Eat with gratitude.

Radiation News

Today the government and TEPCO announce that they have achieved "cold shutdown," meaning that the coolant water must remain under 100 degrees. For now, the "decay heat" has decreased enough to be considered stable. But it takes over two years for the water in a spent fuel pool to cool enough for transfer to storage.

Despite the "stable" temperatures, 11,870 gallons of highly radioactive water leaked from a crack in the desalination unit at Fukushima Daiichi through a gutter into the ocean. The water contained cesium-134 and -137, exceeding the government limits by 267 and 322 times, respectively. Asahi News reported that the water may have contained one million times as much radioactive strontium as the government limit. Dosimeters are now available at DVD rental stores.

Koyu Abe, a Zen Buddhist priest, continues to invite people to dump contaminated soil from their gardens onto the hill behind his temple near Fukushima City. The autumn rice crop may have to be abandoned. Young people are leaving family farms and moving to the city. Thirty-three football fields' worth of contaminated dirt from the no/go zone is looking for a home.

There are only eight nuclear power plants in Japan now operating at the time of this writing. Antinuclear protestors who man the three tents outside the ministry buildings in Tokyo, where we were plied with tea and cookies on a very cold day, say they won't leave until every nuclear power plant has been shut down.

In the United States, the debate over whether to proceed with new nuclear power plants continues. Germany is phasing out all nuclear power, but buying coal from Czechoslovakia, thereby pushing the burden of carbon and methylmercury contamination onto a poorer country.

The Japanese government has passed a law setting age limits on the remaining nuclear power plants. The Institute of Radiological Protection and Nuclear Safety in France estimated that between March and mid-July, 27.1 petabecquerels of cesium-137 leaked into the Pacific Ocean, the greatest amount known to have been released from a single episode. (A petabecquerel is a million billion becquerels.)

The decontamination of towns like Iitate and Minamisōma just outside the exclusion zone gets under way. The cleanup contracts are big business: 40 billion yen is being allocated to Minamisōma alone. Such contracts are deemed a scam, part of the cozy ties between government and the nuclear industry. The workers are uneducated about radiation, questioning as they work whether to remove five or ten centimeters of contaminated soil.

"The Japanese nuclear industry is run so that the more you fail, the more money you receive," said Kiyoshi Sakurai, a nuclear power researcher.

Hirayama's Blog

December 18

Each temporary house group here has a meeting room and social area. Ours is open from 8 a.m. to 5 p.m. Today there were two kids playing. There are kids' books and toys there. It will be Christmas next week. Sometimes we have gatherings and talk in the evenings. The Quilt Club in America offered to send blankets to Kuwagasaki and somebody from the local quilting group gratefully accepted. We received these quilts, filled with hearts and thoughts. Thank you so much! They were shared and given to people in the temp houses and everyone was thrilled. I didn't know blankets could be this warm.

The local quilter's daughter studies music in Paris right now, and she translates my blog into English to share with a Parisian aid organization. She sponsored a charity concert to donate the proceeds to an aid group in Japan. The bond of music spreads from all corners of the world to our region.

On the 13th, Gretel-san, an American writer, came to visit us once again in Kuwagasaki. We first met in June when we were unloading our catch at the Miyako fish market, and this time she came back to talk to us at our newly built prefab shed on the other side of the bay. Thank you for coming all this way and I hope we meet again.

The ties between people. The bonds we share.

I would like to continue spreading information through my blog to show how Tohoku will rebuild itself. We are grateful to all those who have helped.

December 19

Today was the last day of abalone fishing. Freezing morning! The wooden plank on the boat had frozen over with a thick layer of ice. The sea temperature is warmer, so sticking your hand into the water actually warms you up, but once you take your hand out, your body temperature drops again.

Some waves today, and only small abalone. We were able to get the necessary 130, but weight-wise they were not what we had hoped for. Once the abalone are taken to market they are separated between 1st and 2nd class, and the skinny ones get sent back to the sea.

This year's abalone season was over in three hunts.

Urchins were cancelled this year. We thought abalone season might be stopped too, but it wasn't. Next year, between May and August, I hope we'll be able to get urchins again.

December 20

Snow today.

Sea cucumber season has ended and we won't be using the small boats anymore. Tomorrow it may be −5 degrees C— 23 °F—a cold morning. The waves may get rough too.

December 28

Today all temporary houses in Iwate Prefecture received oil heaters for the winter, plus a *kotatsu* table, an electric carpet, an oil stove, and a fan heater.

It's been 292 days since the disaster. Many things have happened to us since then, but somehow we have made it this far with the help of others.

Thank you so much. We will keep working hard toward rebuilding.

Ocean

The ocean is heavy. As the planet took shape, water came from inside the earth. Our litany of natural disasters is nothing compared with the eruptions and earthquakes of the early earth, when the temperature fell to 212 degrees below zero and spewing water vapor condensed into oceans as we know them today.

Ocean bites and butts. Oceans were made from water squeezed out of primordial earth. Later in the making of Earth, water-rich protoplanets crashed here, spilling more liquid.

Morning star—evening star. We live between them, rocking. A rag of cloud keeps wiping away the "I." Drowning, a tiny eye surfaces to take a last look at the ruined earth, at human excesses and defects, and its genius. An ear lifts and hears music.

Water slap, then, *down.* Even underwater I try to see:
   Is the abyss dark or fed by fire?

I hold a cracked tea bowl in my mind. It is lopsided, beautiful, spilling. The chilled depths into which I slide break open like doors. Abyss-san says, "*You have to be alive to die.*"

Morning Sun

Every day we head down the mountain and ply the ruined coast, trying to understand "the void." Our *mikan*—tangerines, in season at this time of year—roll around in the back of the van like little suns.

Snow falls on sun. Steep mountains shoulder clouds, but the storm passes and the winged rafts pull apart and head out to sea. We have the winter solstice on our minds, having gotten past the lunar eclipse, continual earthquakes, and the typhoon; then it will be a new year.

If only the *void* was a shape we could hold in our hands and inspect, turning it over and over until we understood that it is anything but an abandoned warehouse of a world. Quite the opposite: it includes everything that is here. Under us and inside are stochastic events we don't even see: the basaltic lava that flows continuously from undersea rifts; the Kuroshio—Japan's "black current"—warm and northward-flowing, slamming into the cold Bering Sea and spinning counterclockwise; the heaving mantle material pushing the old seafloor aside; the recycling of the lithosphere's slabs into Earth's molten mantle; and the heaving up again.

Death, birth, and renewal are part of Japan's geologic history as well as its cultural sensibility. Every twenty years, the Shinto temples at Ise are torn down completely and rebuilt, exactly as they were. But the pain of loss is excruciatingly real. Who doesn't struggle to come to terms with life's brevity?

A dream resurfaces: the house where I'm sleeping is shaken

hard by a quake, and falls from a cliff. I'm inside. My last view out the window is of a tornado whirling toward me. (Why just one natural disaster per dream, when you can have two?) Hitting bottom, my mind is alert, but I know I'm a ghost, walking with no legs.

Then the van rolls down toward the coast. It lurches and leans. Ahead, winter sun shines on torn water; on crumpled water gates; on remnants—razed houses, grieving households, home-less dogs.

Sun shines on the lonely.

There's sun on red pine islets, on wrecked squid boats whose attractor lights hang like bells with no clappers. Sun on the unlit tunnels through which we hurdle, mountain after mountain, the hooded light at the end saying, "Come, come."

Sun on tangled fishing gear, on the eclipsed moons of black buoys fallen upward from sea to earth.

Sun on snow on sun. On collapsed waves. On bare seafloor. On seawater warmer than air. Faint warmth.

Limpid water-light too thin to hold anything.

* * *

One last swing up a quake-roughened road that hugs the coast, some parts barely navigable. A skiff of snow frosts the high-chambered forest of cedars, and waves shatter on cliffs. Earlier, Kikuchi-san, "the Swimmer," called. We find him on the spot where his family house stood near the water, its footings still marking the layout of rooms. He waves us to a stop and speaks excitedly:

"We just found out that the government will subsidize us for 90 percent of the cost of a fishing boat to replace the ones we lost. I've already picked one out. It's not new, and it needs repairs. I'm going to name it *Rokufukumaru*, a name passed down through three generations. From my grandfather to me. It means Six Happiness, or happiness *times* six. You asked before about hope. There's no such thing as hope . . . At least until we get back on our feet again. But I have a boat coming in the spring . . ."

Traveling south, we enter a blizzard, then the lid of snow lifts as we come into broadening valleys. Thirty hawks descend in a field, fifty snow geese in another. In the samurai town of Tono, Isamu Tatsuno, the founder of the outdoor gear company Mont-bell, has bought land and built a school in what he says will be "a completely green compound, with gardens, wind and solar energy."

Abyss-san says, "One person can do so much good, but the government lies to its people. They are now selling toxic rice from Fukushima Prefecture to developing countries. It's shameful." We keep rolling.

The dosimeter on the console between us reads 0.12.

Millions of dollars of tsunami relief money have been used to support Japan's whaling industry instead of going to refugees. The government is accused by a journalist of "skimming over troublesome truths." The mandate to kill all the animals left behind in the no/go zone is rescinded, but the paperwork to gain entry for the rescues is so complex, one wonders if anyone will wade through it in time to save lives.

The Nuclear Commission says Fukushima Daiichi was unprepared for an emergency of any kind. People who were evacuated from the area around the power plant are calling themselves the "new *hibakusha.*" Rice straw stands in mowed fields like small men in skirts. Rain squalls skip across fields. In Matsuo Bashō's time, a straw cape shielded wandering poet/priests from rain. The itinerant priests I saw in June have ended their peregrinations.

Shounji

Then the rounded head of the Kitakami River shows itself, where it makes a hard bend and goes onet to Ichinomaki. Lumberyards line the narrow lane to Shounji Temple. Alone, I go up on the bank where children died, where ghosts clung to Masumi's back, where the water is aquamarine, and the reeds on both banks are brown stalks clacking together in the breeze.

Two men in a tiny rubber raft ply the reeds, poking the mud with a long stick. Even now, there are thousands of people still missing. Snow geese litter rice fields. A yellow police car creeps slowly down the road, searching for the dead.

The abbot's niece, Fukan-san, greets me. This, the fourth time I've visited, elicits not just the familiar bow, but a hug as well. I've come to see the *bonsho*, the big bell that was brought from the devastated Kannonji Temple up the road to be kept here, and to meet the carpenter who is building the *bonsho*'s shelter. It will be suspended in a wooden stand with a roof decorated with traditional Buddhist carvings.

But first, tea. The temple is unheated. We sit on tatami and warm our hands on teacups near a *tokonoma*, an alcove, with a scroll whose calligraphies translate "Drifting Reed" and "White Cloud."

"There are still so many lost souls here," Fukan-san says, placing little cakes on our plates. She talks of a father in the community who lost both his wife and his child at the Ookawa Elementary School. They found the child's remains and he asked if he could keep her ashes here. "At the funeral for the child he was unable to show emotion. He couldn't greet those neighbors who came, and he was unable to pour the traditional sake. He just sat there, frozen."

There's a group of grieving parents who meet often, but this man never turns up. "He can't bring himself to go to the temporary morgue to find his family. He can't accept that they are dead. A tragedy like that . . . impossible to imagine what it's like . . . the amount of pain and suffering he goes through every day is beyond my imagination. Yet that's my job. To help all of them."

We drink tea in silence. This time, no parents stream through, and no one brings flowers. Nine months have passed. A child's remains are found off the coast of Nobiru: it is "the digger's" child. She and her husband cremate their daughter and give her a proper burial. Determined to help others find their missing children, the mother keeps renting the backhoe, keeps digging. Those who survived the intrusion of tsunami waters on the Kitakami River are getting back to their lives, living with their losses, and fixing up damaged houses and farms.

"I've been thinking about the mysteries of life," Fukan-san says. "We just happen to be born humans. My room is by the toilet and the light is on all night. Big bugs come there and some die. It's nothing when compared to the death of children, and yet, many days I see clearly how we are all equal. I mourn the death of the bugs as well as the children. I tell the parents that those who passed away remind us that we will all die, and to remember this fact; they gave their lives to remind us to live!"

She tells me about the day she went to the river to sit *zazen*, in meditation. "I sat there for a long time," she says. "Then the smell of food cooking wafted up from a farmer's kitchen—such a wonderful smell . . . and it was only then that I cried."

Her head drops, then she gives me a searching look. I nod and tell her that it once happened to me after losing someone I loved;

that food, reminding us of life, stirs grief. Finally, she smiles and jumps to her feet. "Let's go find the carpenter who is building the stand for the Kannonji bell."

The air is brisk. Fukan-san wears a black balaclava and gloves with her robes, white tabi socks and sandals. We rush down the lane to his lumberyard.

"I'm called a *miya daiku,* a master temple builder," Sakai-san says matter-of-factly. In his mid-sixties, he's talkative and hyperenergetic. "I've built 550 temples, and do two or three a year. I'm the first generation. Our family business wasn't doing so well, and they couldn't afford to send us all to high school. My older sister was very clever, so to keep her in school, I went to work and she graduated. I've always loved making things, so I decided to become a craftsman.

"The day I was married, I got up in the middle of the night and went out to the shop and began working. My wife woke and couldn't find me. She called my parents to tell them I'd gone missing. They laughed. 'He's just in his shop. Go back to sleep. That's how he is.'

"I apprenticed to a master from Iwate Prefecture. He moved to Tokyo and I went with him. He'd bought a big piece of land in Tohoku and used the timber from there to make temple carvings. I build the temples with my crew and do all the carvings myself, except for one. A carpenter is not fit to carve a Buddha." (He holds his palms together while saying this, almost absent-mindedly.) "Carving the Buddha is a different world . . . it's like being a priest.

"But since 3/11, I've dedicated my time to those who need help since the disaster. We spent two weeks at Ookawa Elementary School, just up the road, helping the people look for bodies. We brought food to them too. I've been fixing floors that were water-damaged, reconstructing pillars, repairing houses and grave markers. This is what the living have to do at a time like this. But at the end of this year, I must stop, or I'll go broke. We have trucks and heavy equipment and I employ many people who depend on me. So I must start building temples again to pay the bills.

"Do you want to see my tools?" Before we can get our shoes on, he has darted across the road to his lumberyard and shop. Inside are hundreds of boxes of traditional planers, chisels, and saws. "It looks like a mess but no one else uses them. The blades never touch each other. You have to buy these in Kobe. Just three of my best tools are worth enough to buy a new car," he says, flipping open wooden boxes to show us.

"The tools are made by master toolmakers just for temple carving. And my sharpening stone goes back eight hundred years to the Kamakura Period in Kyoto, where a master craftsman said: 'The spirit of the blade lies in the spirit of the natural sharpening tool.' "

We walk to the entryway to the temple to think about where he'll build the "bell house"—an elaborately constructed stand and roof for the great *bonsho*. Fukan-san questions the carpenter about the exact placement. The bronze bell is four feet long and two feet wide and is rung by ramming the end with a long stick. He tells us that during World War II, all the temple bells were taken to be made into weapons. But this bell was spared, and after twenty years it was returned to the Kannonji Temple. "But here it is and we will make a beautiful house for it," he says.

Sakai-san stands in one place and makes the motion of ringing the bell, then another place and tries again. He and Fukan-san laugh. "Well, I'm not sure where to put it yet," he says, looking suddenly distracted, as if remembering all the temples he has yet to build. "But we'll find the right place and make beautiful carvings for it. Maybe it can be built next year . . . or the year after . . . "

Fukan-san looks stunned. She'd hoped it would be completed in a few months. But turning to me she smiles: "You gave us money for this structure. As soon as it is in place, we will have a special ceremony. Some say the sound of the bell signifies *mujo,* impermanence. Others say it is the voice of the Buddha. Whenever the small house is completed, you must come and ring the bell!"

On the Road Again

Abyss-san slides into the seat of the van and turns the key. The engine starts, the heater comes on. We scrape ice from the windshield. He lets the van roll before putting it in gear, takes the twisting road to the top of the mountain, and careens down the other side. No traffic, the dead deer more than half eaten, its carcass a kind of calendar of days: as soon as it's entirely consumed, he says, it's time to leave Japan.

When I close my eyes we fall upward. The shape of the road enters us, the apple orchard, baseball field, and bamboo forest, its branches hanging down and touching ground. A farmer by the side of the road is making charcoal to use as a water purifier. Abyss-san talks a litany of outrages at government corruption; about when he will next distribute donated supplies.

The mind is flung this way and that; the rope of days, braided back into itself, the ends joined, a loop that keeps open the circle of living and dying, morning and evening, night and day. Nikki's sparkling youth and Abyss-san's generosity: beautiful ruptures, openings that delight me in the midst of tragedy. Yet a fisherman we talked to said: "Now there's no happiness in our lives because of the radiation."

We glide over frosted earth, over blunt-cut fields of harvested rice, *sugi* trees bending down to us as if in conversation, their short needles tiny, filigreed, whole forests of green lace. Where trunks have fallen sideways, we drive on heartwood—smooth, smooth—bumping across rice fields and water ditches, we pierce each small farm as we go, cutting through leafless persimmon trees hung with orange orbs. "All those moons," Nikki says. Lopped in half.

We cross a river, our velocity splitting open the valley like a peach. Buckled roads fall to either side of the van, and smoke from debris piles fades into dusk, or is it morning? Lights from the vanquished town of Rikuzentakata come on, as if from nonexistent houses. A brief twinkling, then the illusion fades, the town's desolation cut, the two halves identical, their tidal monotonies and rubbish-glutted shores, all the pines but one, pulled like tooth.

We're falling. Forward now, not down. Open. Away from what is broken. To slice is to heal. We enter the ocean, rapt and wakeful, its rough grain cracking open, the van moving north and south at once, the Wave falling on either side of the blade.

Ikoji

We stop a last time at Ikoji, the small temple with the kindergarten in Shichigahama. The abbot trained at Daitokuji, Japan's most famous Rinzai Buddhist monastery in northern Kyoto. Practice there is very tough, but the results can be like polished silver: its graduates exude a sourceless deep shine.

The abbot bursts through the door, tall and big-boned with a wide smile and large ears. Sometimes a person's presence can change a room, and make it suddenly feel larger. He stands, then sits, and at every moment he radiates without a radiator. He slides his arm around his wife, smiling. With me, he's brisk, kind, direct, and informal.

We sit facing each other. My note-taking hand shakes—that's what his presence does to me. He waits patiently until I can talk. There's a fly on my cheek and I wonder if I should flick it away. I don't. For his wife it's the end of a long day taking care of children and she leans affectionately against him.

"Usually people don't come here," he begins. "This place is hard to find," he says, and laughs. "And you've been here twice already!" He gives the child who is waiting for his mother a kind look. "Once a tsunami comes you should never run back to get something. You have to give it all up on the spot," he says. His wife passes a box of chocolates. They take turns picking out a sweet. The boy sits quietly, shyly, chewing candy and holding a ball.

The abbot continues: "We thought we were safe from the tsunami. See, there are mountains all around protecting us from the ocean. But it came right through that gap." He points to a notch in the hills.

"I had to face it. I had to face the wave coming when we didn't expect it, and in that moment I knew I had to survive so I could help others. I was very concerned about the woman who had gone back to her house. I was yelling over and over, 'Come back, come to the mountain with us.' I waited until the last moment when everyone had to leave. I prayed aloud for her to go to the *nikai*, the second floor of her house. Then one of her neighbors informed me that her house had only one floor!" He laughs.

"We had already gone up to the top of the hill with the children and the staff, but I kept hearing noises and not understanding what it was. I heard stones being thrown and something banging. I yelled out, 'Who is it?' A wavering voice came back: 'It's me!'

"I knew it was her—the woman we couldn't find. She had climbed to the temple roof and was banging on it with rocks and tree branches. I ran down the mountain. I rescued her from the wall behind the temple, put her on my back, and carried her up to the top of the hill. Finally we were all safe. Later, hours after the last wave had receded, we became very cold and hungry. Our clothes were wet and it was below freezing, so I went back down the hill and got some food. This whole room, here in the kindergarten, was mostly under water. But I knew there were some snacks and juices here in the uppermost shelves, so I waded through—the water was up to my neck—and got them, and carried them back up to the others. We shared the food. There wasn't much but it helped.

"It was snowing and we were getting hypothermic. I thought a long time about how to get warm. There are traditions in Japan about one's ancestors. They are thought to live inside these tall pieces of wood called *ihai* with the names of the dead written on them. It's very important for families to have these memorial sticks. They are sacred. But we had to survive. I ran down the hill again and waded through the water to the cemetery by our temple. I had made the decision to take the *ihai* from the graves and break them up to use for firewood! This is considered a sacrilege, but I'd thought very hard about it and decided it was the best thing to do."

A long silence. His wife muffles a raspy in-breath. "We've been laughing a lot . . . I don't know why!" she says. The abbot looks at her, his eyebrows raised, and he smiles. She whispers again: "My husband was upset because his golf clubs got ruined when the water came into our house!" We all laugh out loud. "The tatami in the temple has been replaced for the second time in six months," she continues. "But the autumn flowers that line the stone paths still bloom."

I get up and look out the window. Darkness is coming on and just as the sun vanishes, it begins raining very hard. The rice field in front of the temple is still waterlogged from the typhoon, and the ruined car is lying in it, nose up, as if trying to suck in oxygen. Rain turns to snow. At Daitokuji practitioners sit in meditation facing the wall. Facing emptiness and then no emptiness. The box of candy is passed again, as if each brown square stood for the present, and by eating them we could face whatever comes.

The abbot speaks, his voice solemn now. "Since the disaster, some older people have committed suicide. But there's no reason to do that. We just start from where we are, from whatever the day brings to us." He leans forward, resting his elbows on his knees, and looks straight at me: "The tsunami is past. We must think about the future. What we will do next. Up on the mountain my wife and I decided to restart the kindergarten as soon as possible. The children may say that they lost their house, or their lunch box, or someone they loved, but it's always followed with laughter. It's hard for adults to hear these things, but we try to remain energetic and happy. It helps us. In disasters, children show us the way to laughter. They are our special treasures."

As he glances at the scalloped hills, at the smooth notches where the waves burst through and rushed toward the temple, his eyelids flicker as thoughts skitter through. He turns to me. When he smiles his ears move and his teeth shine. He speaks slowly: "The tsunami isn't important. There was no Wave."

Epilogue

White clouds: void is form.
Red leaves form is void.
White clouds and red leaves—
All swept away by an evening's wind.

—KODOJIN

The ocean holds the streams of stories. The Wave came to carry them, empty them of meaning. The power of the water pulling back, baring the ocean floor, took all the loose ends, the beginnings and endings, and unraveled them, recomposing stories so they had no familiar shapes. Some were all endings with no middles; others were so shapeless there was no way to tell how they had started or if they could end.

The Wave was center and fringe at once, a totality, both destructive and beautiful. Oceans of story were taken up by it. Roof beams and window frames were whittled back into the trees from which they came. The furrowed ocean cleaved land, and knifed the wavering ribbons of each human and animal story.

Masumi writes to tell me that her great-uncle Satoru and great-aunt Satsuko have rebuilt their house and are living there. A winter vegetable and flower garden was planted again. Kazuyoshi and Kayuko have not yet decided where to rebuild, but they are growing vegetables on Grandmother's land, though they will not be allowed to rebuild her house.

* * *

Dream: I was given a book of the names of the dead so I would be sure to spell them correctly in both Kanji and English. In return I made a book of the living and gave it back to them, of those who faced the Wave and died, of those who learned to live.

At the end of December snow geese and hawks tumble down and inhabit rice fields. There is still this kind of bounty. My dreams continue: Nikki, Abyss-san, and I circumnavigate a standing dead cedar. We are tethered to the trunk on a loose line and spin round and round, but the harness is not so loose that we can drift away. We are alive and glad of it; we are lively despite being sad. We see how pain and joy are not opposites, but spark off each other. We can see the pain of loss and swing the other way, encountering the unexpected joy of survival.

All human lives are lonely journeys. When the moon shines on "worried water," what Buddhists call "a sudden path" becomes clear. We don't think, we just take it, no matter where it leads. We are fearful and fearless at the same time. The body moves, the boat lifts up and over the double wave-front, and lunges down into trough after trough. We keep going, despite the urgent desire to return to those we love, to what we know. Snow comes in fat flakes. We experience hot and cold simultaneously. Time has vanished. We can't see.

At intervals we are terrified, angry, and bewildered. We wonder if we'll fall through the hull of the boat or sink to the bottom of the sea. Nothing feels solid. We want to grasp at something, but it's too late. Our hands are cold. We keep stepping into wild places.

The boat nods, lunges, and rocks from side to side; the body is pushed and pulled. Water pours in orifices, shoots through scuppers, and we know that it's fruitless to maintain security because "form is empty," which means there are no walls. Even underwater our eyes have opened wide: everything is possible: the ways out and the ways in are both open doors.

For two days and two nights we rock and roll in nothingness, in no-man's-ocean, between sets of waves. Will there be another tsunami? How can anyone know? We wait. Our former sense of time was driven by desire; now we have none, which is freedom. We aren't even fleeing; we are completely absorbed.

Form is emptiness; emptiness is form. Nothing about those words is nihilistic. Quite the opposite. When there's talk about emptiness—which is the same thing as form—it means "noth-ingness" in the sense that there are no preconceptions, no expec-tations, no versions of this and that, no prejudice, no bias, no denials, no delusions. Seen this way, the void includes every-thing.

From the boat we can see in all directions. A 360-degree view. The lonely journey is not one of solitude. It's taken along with everyone else. We are alone but adjacent, linked, cantilevered, part of the riprap. We carry the dead and they carry us. There is solace in that, not fear.

Some fishermen took their boats out; others were totally im-mersed in the surging and retreating waters of the Wave. All such trips were difficult, and the experience of those hours and days can never be communicated fully. We try and no expres-sion quite gets to the heart of it, so we become lonely all over again.

It's been almost a year. Now "worried water" has receded and a calm ocean has taken its place. The ocean carries living fish and dead humans in a single embrace. No longer rushing back and surging forward, it jostles in place and makes its tidal rounds as usual. The tectonic plates have grown quieter. The 375-foot-long seismic rip will heal. But geologists remind us that Earth was simply "recycling" its subsiding plate into the crust, that another massive movement will occur and the jarred seismic zone will displace another mountain of water and send it shoreward. There's a 70 percent chance that a big one will hit Tokyo.

Along the coast road the brown watermark hits a hundred feet up, staining cedar trees brown, reminding us of what water can do, of its immense and indiscriminate power. Great white egrets flock in the trees that line the Kitakami River; an ocean breeze drives whitecaps curling back toward some azure center.

Buddhists say, "There is no ignorance and no extinction of ignorance." The moon glides into Earth's shadow, swims out again. Everything uncertain is striding. Snow fell on the day the disaster occurred; snow falls again today.

PERSONS (IN ORDER OF APPEARANCE)

Kikuchi, "the Swimmer"—fisherman, Kamaishi
Yajima Masumi—interpreter, guide
Yajima Kazuko—Masumi's mother
Yajima Saburo—Masumi's father
Grandmother—Masumi's grandmother, Kazuko's mother
Otomo Kazuyoshi—Masumi's uncle, Kazuko's brother
Sachiko—driver, friend of Masumi
The abbot—Zenoji Temple
Mrs. Watanabe—the abbot's wife, Ikoji Temple
Tenku Ruff—American Buddhist nun, friend of Fukan-san
Fukan-san—Buddhist nun, the abott's niece, Shounji Temple
The abbot—Shounji Temple
Nikki Kininmonth—interpreter, guide, translator
Atsuchi Kanno, "Abyss-san"—driver, guide
Hanaoka Wakao—Greenpeace campaigner, Tokyo
Hirayama—father, fisherman, Miyako
Hirayama Masayuki—son, fisherman, Miyako
Ito Tsuyako, "Ito-san"—geisha, Kamaishi
Satoshi—nephew of Ito-san, architect
Maruki Hiroyuki—sake merchant, Kamaishi
Elizabeth Oliver—founder of ARK, animal rescuer, Sasayama
Henry Tricks—bureau chief, *The Economist,* Tokyo
Narui Mayuko—animal rescuer, Tokyo
Utsumi Kumezo—retired fisherman, Katsura Island
Mori—boatman, Matsushima Bay
Jin—shaman, photographer

Great-Uncle Satoru—Masumi's great-uncle, Kazuko's uncle
Great-Aunt Satsuko—Masumi's great-aunt, Kazuko's aunt
Otomo Kayuko—Masumi's aunt
Pico Iyer—writer and friend, Nara
Hiroko—Pico's wife
Reiko-san—friend of Tenku Ruff's, Ofunato
Sakai-san—temple carpenter
The abbot—Ikoji Temple, Shichigahama

Acknowledgments

It is impossible to thank enough those in Japan who participated in the making of this book at a time so difficult and bewildering. I wish to thank Masumi and her entire family: her parents, Kazuko and Saburo; her uncle and aunt, Kazuyoshi and Kayuko; her great-uncle and great-aunt, Satoru and Satsuko; and her grandmother, for inviting me into their homes and lives, and allowing me to hear their stories.

Thanks to those who faced the Wave and all the ongoing hardships: Fukan-san, the Buddhist nun; the Abbot of Ikoji Temple and his wife; Hirayama-san and his father; Kikuchi-san, "the Swimmer"; Ito-san, the geisha, and her nephew, Satoshi-san; the sake merchant who saved her life, Hiroyuki-san. Thanks to the islanders, Kumezo-san, the hip-hop gang, and Mori. Thanks to Jin. Thanks to Reiko-san and Sakai-san, and to the fishermen who wished to remain anonymous.

Special thanks to my guide, interpreter, translator, and pal on the road, Nikki, and to "Abyss-san," for his hospitality, his curry, his keen eye and ear, and his superb driving.

Deep thanks to the courageous rescuers of animals abandoned during the disaster, especially Elizabeth Oliver, Henry Tricks, Mayu, and everyone at Dogwood and Hisaiba.

Thanks to Shin'ya Hagio and to Sachiko, and others along the way who gave kind help.

My gratitude for dear friends: Pico Iyer and Hiroko; Leila Phillip, with whom thoughts about this book originated; my Wyoming neighbors Rita and Jamie, Thekla and Callum, and Robert Palmquist. Three bows to Buddhist monks and nuns who helped me, especially Michael Wenger and Tenku Ruff. In memory of the early years living in the household of Chogyam Trungpa Rinpoche, whose teachings on the bardo at the 1971 Allenspark Seminar instruct me still.

Without the love, moral support, and laughter of my companion, Neal Conan, I'd still be wandering in the bardo.

Thanks, finally, to my distinguished editor, Dan Frank, for his wisdom, generosity, and humor, and to my loyal agent, Liz Darhansoff. My writing life with them has endured for almost thirty years.

While traveling from mountain to shore on the northeast coast of Japan, I wrote several poems that appear in this book, and later, undertook my own translations of Matsuo Bashō's poems. Any mistakes made in those renderings of his fine poems are all mine.

Bibliography

Aitken, Robert. *A Zen Wave*. New York: Weatherhill, 1995.

Beckett, Samuel. *Stories and Texts for Nothing*. New York: Grove Press, 1967.

Berger, John. *Hold Everything Dear*. New York: Pantheon Books, 2007.

Blacker, Carmen. *The Catalpa Bow*. London: George Allen & Unwin, 1986.

Bush, Susan. *The Literati on Painting: Su Shih to Tung Ch'i-ch'ang*. Cambridge, Mass.: Harvard University Press, 1971.

Calasso, Roberto. *Ka*. New York: Alfred A. Knopf, 1998.

Eliot, T. S. *Collected Poems 1909–1962*. New York: Harcourt, Brace & World, 1970.

Foster, Nelson, and Jack Shoemaker. *The Roaring Stream*. Hopewell, N.J.: Ecco Press, 1996.

Guenther, Herbert, and Chogyam Trungpa. *The Dawn of Tantra*. Berkeley: Shambhala, 1975.

Hearn, Lafcadio. *Japan, An Interpretation*. Rutland, Vt.: Charles Tuttle, 1962.

Hori Ichiro. *Folk Religion in Japan*. Chicago: University of Chicago Press, 1974.

Hough, Susan Elizabeth. *Earthshaking Science*. Princeton, N.J.: Princeton University Press, 2002.

Keene, Donald, ed. *Anthology of Japanese Literature*. New York: Grove Press, 1960.

———. *Appreciations of Japanese Culture*. Tokyo: Kodansha International, 1981.

———. *Seeds in the Heart, A History of Japanese Literature*. Vol. 1. New York: Henry Holt, 1993.

Kodojin. *Old Taoist*. Translation and commentary by Stephen Addiss. New York: Columbia University Press, 2000.

Lao Tzu. *Taoteching*. Translation by Red Pine. San Francisco: Mercury House, 1996.

Lowell, Percival. *Occult Japan*. Boston: Houghton-Mifflin, 1894.

Makoto Ueda. *Matsuo Bashō*. Tokyo: Kodansha International, 1982.

Matsuo Bashō. *Bashō, The Complete Haiku*. Translation by Jane Reichhold. Tokyo: Kodansha International, 2008.

————. *The Narrow Road to Oku*. Translation by Donald Keene. Tokyo: Kodansha International, 1996.

————. *The Narrow Road to the Deep North and Other Travel Sketches*. Translation by Nobuyuki Yuasa. New York: Penguin Books, 1966.

McKinney, Meredith. *The Tale of Saigyo*. Ann Arbor: Center for Japanese Studies, University of Michigan Press, 1998.

National Oceanic and Atmospheric Administration (NOAA) Website.

Parker, Bruce. *The Power of the Sea*. New York: Macmillan, 2010.

Pine, Red, trans. *The Heart Sutra*. Washington, D.C.: Shoemaker & Hoard, 2004.

Sato Hiroaki, and Burton Watson, trans. *From the Country of Eight Islands*. New York: Columbia University Press, 1986.

Shodo Harada, Roshi. *Morning Dewdrops of the Mind*. Berkeley, Calif.: North Atlantic Books/Frog, 1993.

Shunryu Suzuki, Roshi. *Branching Streams Flow in the Darkness*. Berkeley: University of California Press, 1999.

————. *Not Always So*. New York: HarperCollins, 2002.

Tanizaki Jun'ichiro. *In Praise of Shadows*. London: Jonathan Cape, 1991.

Trefil, James. *A Scientist at the Seashore*. New York: Dover, 1984.

Trungpa, Chogyam. *The 1971 Allenspark Seminar: "The Bardo"* (personal notes).

————. *Transcending Madness*. Boston: Shambhala, 1992.

Walcott, Derek. *Omeros*. New York: Farrar, Straus & Giroux, 1990.

About the Author

Gretel Ehrlich, one of the preeminent and most admired observers of the natural world, is the author of fifteen books, including *The Solace of Open Spaces*, *A Match to the Heart*, and *This Cold Heaven*, for which she received the PEN New England, Henry David Thoreau Award for Nature Writing. She is the recipient of an award from the American Academy of Arts and Letters, and a Guggenheim Fellowship, among many others. Her work has been widely anthologized, including in *Best Essays of the Century*. Since 1993, she has traveled many times by dogsled with subsistence Inuit hunters on the sea ice of northwestern Greenland. She lives in Wyoming.

www.gretel-ehrlich.com

A Note on the Type

The type used in this book was designed by Pierre Simon Fournier *le jeune*. In 1764 and 1766 he published his *Manuel typographique*, a treatise on the history of French types and printing, and on what many consider his most important contribution to typography—the measurement of type by the point system.

Composed by North Market Street Graphics,
Lancaster, Pennsylvania

Printed and bound by Berryville Graphics,
Berryville, Virginia